Demystifying SaaS-based PLM:
Cloud, PLM and Life After COVID

Michael Finocchiaro

Many thanks to the folks that agreed to interviews and were ever so patient with my follow-up questions for this white paper: Steve Dertien, Greg Payne, Walid Saad, and François Lamy of PTC; Denis Goudstikker, Jamie Wilkins, and Kerri Doyle of Siemens Digital Industries Software; Mark Reisig and Bruce Bookbinder of Aras Solutions; Max Behre and Mark Wenske of Dassault Systèmes; Oleg Shilovitsky of BeyondPLM and OpenBOM; Srinath Jonnalagadda of Autodesk; Tom Shoemaker and Kevin Crothers of Propel; James White and Tesa Laslavic of Upchain; Håkan Karden and Torbjörn Holm of Eurostep; Ralf Seidler and Marco Rembold of Schwindt; Yoann Maingon of Ganister; Stan Przybylinski of CIMDATA; Marc Halpern of Gartner Group; Lionel Gréalou of xLifecycle; Rob Ferrone of Quick Release; Ron Close of Shapr3D;Stephan Clambaneva of iD8trs; Christophe Maisonnave of HPE; and Sebastien Mercier-Masseaux.

I'd also like to thank Damian Navas, Simon Warren, Lucy Carey and the rest of the **"To Cloud Crowd"** team at Haig & Co for their support of this project.

EXECUTIVE SUMMARY

Cloud has been a hot topic in Product Lifecycle Management (PLM) for quite some time. With the onset of the COVID-19 pandemic, this movement will accelerate as companies move forward their digital initiatives to minimize physical contact while increasing collaboration. This book will talk briefly about the history of PLM and cloud computing and attempt to dispel some myths about cloud that are commonly circulating. It will talk about today's SaaS PLM platforms. I will then give some pros and cons of leveraging cloud technologies before giving you a list of self-assessment questions about the risks involved in moving your PLM to the cloud.

Some of the topics will include:
- Security in the Cloud
- Vendor Lock-In
- Cloud Economics
- Current Cloud Platforms from the Major PLM Vendors
- Cloud Strengths and Cloud Challenges

Target Audience: PLM Deciders, IT Managers, CTOs of Manufacturing companies

TABLE OF CONTENTS

Figures

Tables

Part 1 – Introduction and Background

To Cloud or Not to Cloud

Cloud-based PLM has been a hot topic for much of the recent past, and despite the liters (or gallons for you non-metric readers) of ink dispensed already, I wanted to chime in with my own thoughts and experiences. I published a few articles already on LinkedIn about **3D**EXPERIENCE and cloud[1], but I wanted here to give a more detailed analysis of the pros and cons of cloud and PLM in general. Caveat emptor: There is a bit more detail on **3D**EXPERIENCE platform and DS below just because it was one of the first vendors to launch PLM on the cloud and I worked on that launch[2], my knowledge of that platform is quite broad and deep. I did, however, try to include as much information about the other PLM vendors when that information was available publicly and conducted interviews with representatives of many PLM vendors (see the Thank you section at the top of this document).

The "To Cloud" Crowd

Many companies have begun to look seriously at cloud for a multitude of factors. Perhaps the first factor is cost: they feel that moving from a front-loaded capital expenditure (capex) to a subscription-based operating expenses (opex) system gives them more flexibility and allows them more freedom with their cashflow. They also feel they can significantly reduce IT and facilities expenses by sunsetting local machine rooms and data centers. The idea that there will be no ceiling to scalability due to the elasticity of the distributed cloud computing model is also a highly seductive aspect in favor of cloud. Finally, the factor of peer pressure is also non-negligible as the cloud buzzword has been in the business press headlines for several years now and is often mentioned in conjunction with other buzzwords like "Industry 4.0[3]", "digital thread", and "digital twin[4]" creating misunderstandings as to what all these terms actually mean. Other enterprise software functions such as HR and CRM have moved to cloud, so why not PLM?

The "Not To Cloud" Crowd

Then you have the folks that are extremely reluctant to move to cloud. The primary objection is fear: fear for the security of their data. If it is on the cloud, isn't it more vulnerable to hackers and industrial espionage? There is also always justifiable fear of change in general: if it works, don't fix it. Another legitimate fear is vendor lock-in: if I want to change platforms, will I be able to get my data out of the cloud? Lastly, there are also those who feel that cloud is a fad and that the pendulum will swing back to on-premises once enough people get burned by their failed cloud implementations.

---

[1] https://www.linkedin.com/pulse/demystifying-3dexperience-cloud-michael-finocchiaro

[2] I worked for Dassault Systèmes from 2010 to 2017 and was on the **3D**EXPERIENCE launch team from 2014 to 2017 as the Global Architect. See my LinkedIn profile, https://www.linkedin.com/in/mfinocchiaro/ and the About the Author section at the end of this white paper.

[3] See https://en.wikipedia.org/wiki/Fourth_Industrial_Revolution

[4] See my article about Demystifying Digital Thread and Digital Twins on LinkedIn, https://www.linkedin.com/pulse/demystifying-digital-dilemmas-michael-finocchiaro/)

The Truth Is Out There

Neither of these two clubs has all the answers and both are asking the right questions. The rest of this white paper will try to address each of these objections and ask additional questions in order to help managers demystify the various decision factors around whether moving PLM to cloud is the right thing for their organization. Let's first look at the PLM market and its approach to cloud.

A Short History of PLM

Product Lifecycle Management has evolved enormously during my 30 years of working on innovation and product development. Initially conceived for airplanes and cars, computer-aided design (CAD) and computer-aided manufacturing (CAM) were used to make computer models of the product being designed (now rebaptized "digital twins"). Three-dimensional (3D) modeling soon became the norm, meaning larger more complex files which required sophisticated systems for storing the large CAD models. This was baptized Product Data Management (PDM). And once many engineers wanted to work simultaneously on the same assembly, the digitalization of change management, part classification, project and program management, and digital mockup among other engineering processes all created a need for a database to store usernames, change orders, parts libraries, and all the other metadata, or data about the 3D geometry files and their governance models. This was called Product Lifecycle Management (PLM) (see Figure 1). Once the data became unwieldy and diverse, indexation servers were required to search through the mountains of information. What you ended up with was application servers on the front end, databases, index servers and file servers on the backend and a lot of headaches when it came to migration, patching and upgrades.

It is also important to note the interdependencies of PLM on other enterprise software such as Enterprise Resource Planning (ERP). As shown in an example in Figure 2, we are making a product for a supermarket that is in the Consumer Packaged Goods (CPG) industry. The items in the upper right called "Design Intent" are typically managed inside the PLM system where the design is mastered, whereas the factory, warehousing and operations shown here as "Manufacturing Intent" are all typically managed by the ERP system. **The interlinking of the two is essential to ensuring smooth operations of the company. In the new parlance, it is usually called "Digital Thread" because it is supposed to demonstrate the superiority of digital connections between systems that avoid manual breakdowns or lost documents.** Naturally, the same analogy could be made in any other industry.

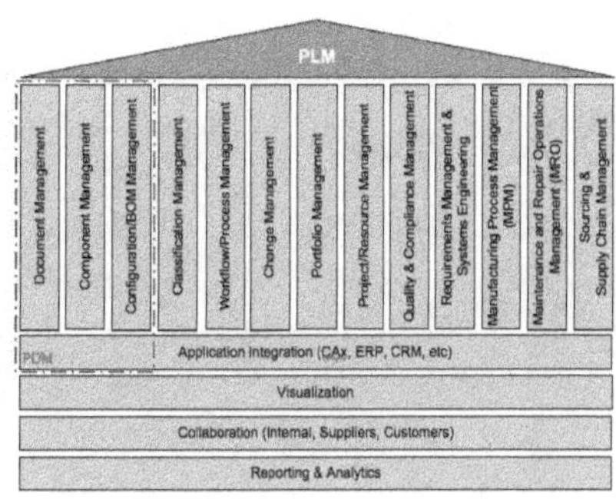

Figure 1 - PDM and PLM Functionalities (from http://BeyondPLM.com)

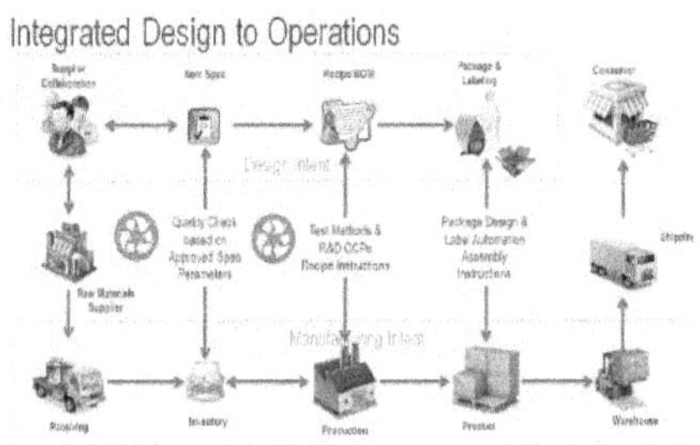

Figure 2 - Illustration of Design vs Manufacturing in a Consumer Packaged Goods (CPG) product (from https://www.linkedin.com/pulse/what-plm-mes-erp-raymond-wodar/)

PLM systems such as Dassault Systèmes VPM, MatrixOne, Sherpa, UGS Unigraphics, SDRC Metaphase, PTC Pro/INTRALINK and Pro/PDM, Computervision (CV) OPTEGRA, Autodesk AutoCAD Vault among others tried to capitalize on these initiatives. One obscure company, called Windchill, was created by ex-SDRC veterans James Hepplemann and John Gibson who started writing a Java-based toolbox that was being considered by CV as an OPTEGRA replacement. All of these deployments required relatively large computer servers and storage and were sometimes relegated to the dark, blinking machine rooms running the enterprise resource management (ERP) software, which was already running the factories, the procurement processes, human resources, billing, etc. Sometimes, they were installed in an abandoned cubicle. Since the deployment was so heavy in defining data models and adapting the systems to existing business processes, it was not uncommon for the IT aspects to be overlooked while the business units were busy deploying and customizing the system. This led to performance issues and frustration for users and management as deployment schedules became months or years instead of weeks. Also, with an ERP, business line management can point to reduction in inventory or reduced cost in manufacturing to justify the required investment IT. **The financial benefits are far harder to quantify with PLM and it was often seen as a toy for engineers rather than a powerful platform for increasing design and production efficiency.** Figure 3 below summarizes the major acquisitions of the three primary billion dollar PLM vendors.

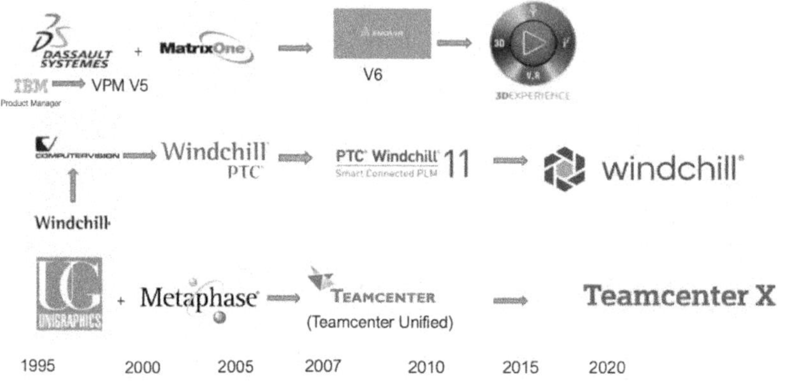

Figure 3 - Acquisitions and Brand History the PLM Billion Dollar Club (minus Autodesk)

During the '90s and '00s, there was a massive amount of consolidation in the industry: EDS purchased SDRC[5] and merged it with Unigraphics to create Teamcenter and spun off as UGS[6] which itself was later acquired by Siemens[7]; PTC bought Computervision (CV)[8] who in the meantime had acquired a minority stake in Windchill - Windchill quickly replaced Pro/INTRALINK, Pro/PDM as PTC's flagship PLM platform; Dassault Systèmes (DS) bought MatrixOne[9] and merged it with VPM (a byproduct of their adaptation of IBM Product Manager and their long alliance with IBM) to create V6[10], later rebranded **3D**EXPERIENCE. Each of these companies also made massive acquisitions in the '10s to expand towards manufacturing (the purchase of Tecnomatix by UGS and subsequent merge into Teamcenter; DENEB, EAI-Delta and Safework were acquired by Dassault to create the DELMIA brand; simulation (Dassault purchased ABAQUS to create the SIMULIA brand, Siemens purchased LMS to create SimCenter; Autodesk purchased NEi NASTRAN to create Inventor Nastran), and, most recently, the internet of things (IOT) with PTC's purchase of ThingWorx (see Figures 4 through 6 below for examples) Oracle purchased Eigner&Partners E6 and created the on-premises PDM platform Agile. After creating Oracle Cloud, they created a subset of the Supply Chain Management solution dedicated to Product Lifecycle Management. Meanwhile, Autodesk moved beyond their pervasive 2D package AutoCAD and created Autodesk Vault for their PDM platform and introduced Autodesk Inventor as their 3D CAD system. They are overwhelmingly present in the Construction space which was redubbed Building Information Management (BIM), but have also been present in certain aspects of the product development space as well.

---

[5] https://www.designnews.com/eds-acquire-sdrc-take-ugs-private
[6] https://www.cadalyst.com/collaboration/product-lifecycle-management/news/eds-sells-ugs-plm-solutions-205-billion-11323
[7] https://www.plm.automation.siemens.com/global/de/our-story/newsroom/siemens-press-release/43058
[8] https://www.crunchbase.com/acquisition/parametric-technology-acquires-computervision--e74ae6c6
[9] https://www.3ds.com/press-releases/single/dassault-systemes-to-acquire-matrixone/
[10] https://www.3ds.com/press-releases/single/dassault-systemes-introduces-v6-to-the-market/

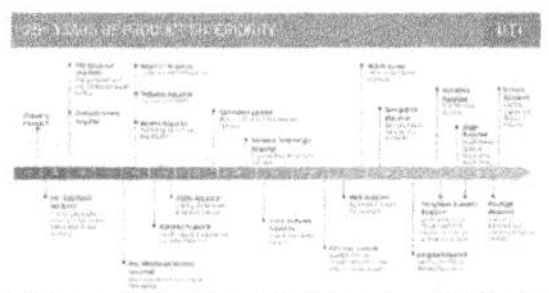

Figure 4 - PTC Acquisition History (to 2020)

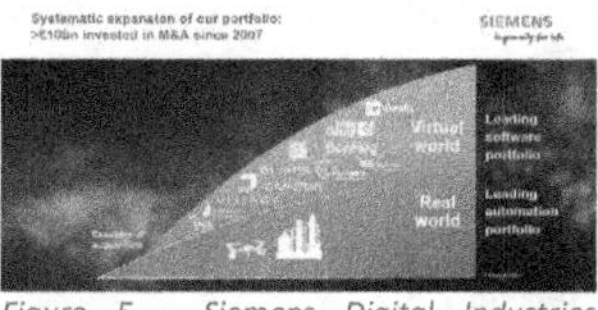

Figure 5 - Siemens Digital Industries Software Acquisition History (up to 2016)

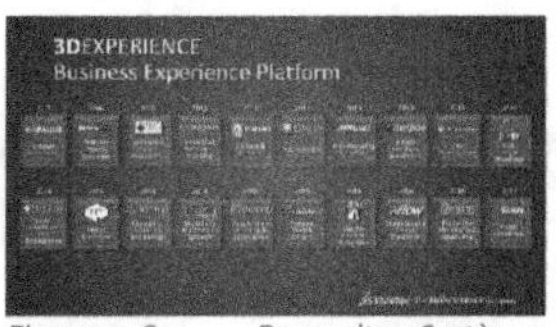

Figure 6 - Dassault Systèmes Acquisition History (to 2017)

This consolidation in the PLM software industry expanded the footprint from just CAD data management towards managing the entire upstream and downstream development processes from conception to fabrication, what has more recently been relabeled as "digital thread" or "digital continuity." This also meant from an IT point of view that PLM complexity increased exponentially as the data models became infinitely more sophisticated with increasing number of external systems needed to be integrated to exchange data with PLM. Companies started to look for ways to reduce their IT spend and offload the complexities of migration, patching, integrations, and upgrades to external partners so that rather than spending 20-30% (or more) of their time **MANAGING** the PLM system, and spend more of their time actually **USING** it and seeing the potential gains (time to market, innovation acceleration, improved quality, etc.) that the vendors promised.

One last thing to keep in mind is that what started out as an expensive niche solution for the aerospace and automotive industries quickly applied to other industries as well. Companies that manufacture heavy machinery and industrial equipment, agricultural equipment, cruise ships, energy, powerplants, oil platforms, circuit boards, and consumer electronics all became very interested in the potential savings from PLM. Soon, high-tech, pharmaceuticals, consumer goods, fashion and retail, construction and engineering, and many other industries adopted PLM as well. **Some of these new industries did not have a tradition of heavy IT skills and this became a barrier to adoption due to the implicit complexities in PLM deployments.**

Short History of PLM Cloud Offerings

In order to respond to this expressed desire to outsource PLM and to address the newer industries, the PLM vendors all started to look into simplifying deployment of the systems. One of the very first online PLM systems was BOM.com which changed its name to Arena Solutions in 2003, but it remained a niche player as few companies were willing to move their PLM online.

In 2005, PTC and IBM teamed up to create Windchill PDMLink On Demand with perhaps the market's first multi-tenant PLM with full CAD integration. In other words, there was a single Windchill instance serving multiple clients, but since the code is shared, individual customizations of the system are severely limited. It grew to nearly 100 customers, but there was frustration due to the limitations in customization imposed by multi-tenant systems. The alternative for PTC customers was to leverage partners such as NetIDEAS and their PaaS offerings for Windchill managed services. PTC acquired NetIDEAS in 2013 and, as we will see later, it will become part of the foundation for the new PTC Atlas platform announced in mid-2020.

Early in the '10s, there were several perfunctory approaches to PLM on the cloud from longtime PLM heavyweights Dassault and Autodesk such as the ill-fated PLM Express and n!Volve suites from Dassault and the similarly stillborn PLM 360 from Autodesk both from back around 2011 to 2013. Were they both too early to the market or was the flop due to positioning or product gaps? Probably a little of each. Dassault's suite was excessively CATIA-centric, had little or no BOM or Change Management, and as such was rejected by their customer base. As for Autodesk, they had a PR mess due to CEO Carl Bass's dissing of PLM in years[11] past which they had to walk back. PLM 360 was essentially a mashup of about 12 acquisitions including Datastay which was their new core. However, when one looked under the hood, there was a lack of depth in each of the solutions and a true lack of connectivity between them which was an inhibitor to sales.

State of the Market 2020

Fast forward several years and now the largest vendors, PTC, Dassault Systèmes, Siemens Digital Industry Software, and Autodesk (all worth over US$1B and thus referred to in this document as the Billion Dollar Club) have revamped and repositioned their cloud offerings. **3D**EXPERIENCE platform was launched on DS Public Cloud in 2015, PLM 360 was rebranded as Autodesk Fusion Lifecycle, Siemens recently launched Teamcenter X as a cloud-native platform, and PTC purchased Onshape and has announced a forthcoming Atlas platform as a SaaS backend. Aras Innovator has always been cloud-ready and is preparing a pure-SaaS offering for the near future. Add to this mix smaller PLM solutions such as Propel PLM, Arena Solutions, and OpenBOM, and there is quite a lot of choice for customers looking at cloud-readiness or SaaS deployments for their PLM. Each of these will be discussed separately at the end of this white paper. It should be added that in order to more specifically incite the massive SOLIDWORKS user base to **3D**EXPERIENCE platform, in 2019, Dassault introduced a complete suite of products stemming from their ENOVIA and DELMIA brands on the cloud rebranded as **3D**EXPERIENCE WORKS - all fully optimized for use with SOLIDWORKS. Figures 7 through 10 show the portfolios of the four biggest PLM vendors.

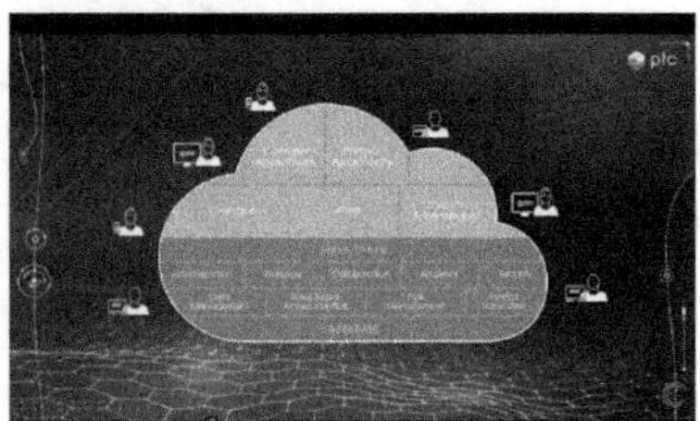

Figure 7 - PTC Atlas Announcement (June 2020)

Figure 8 - Teamcenter X Announcement (June 2020)

Figure 9 - 3DEXPERIENCE WORKS Portfolio (2019)

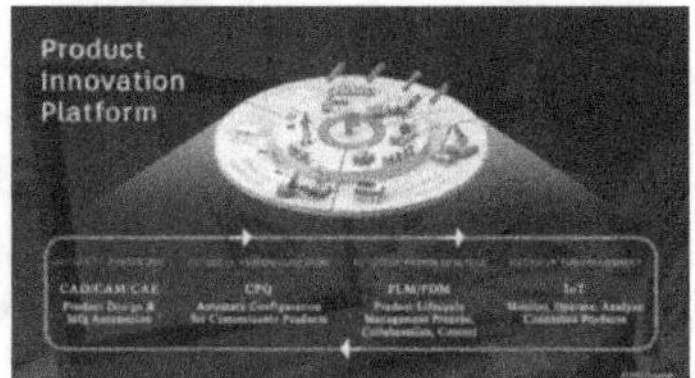

Figure 10 - Autodesk Product Innovation Platform Portfolio (2016)

Oddly, however, despite all this effort, the big money is still being made primarily on-premises. Why is that?

A Brief History of PLM and Cloud, Part 1 (IaaS and PaaS)

Let's step back a moment and think about the history of Cloud-based PLM. The first move from a dark, dusty server room in the company basement was outsourcing the servers to a hosting partner, in other words Infrastructure as a Service (IaaS). This did not fundamentally change how PLM operated, other than reducing cost (electricity, water cooling, air conditioning, etc.) via delegating the physical hardware and its management to a 3rd party. If you think about how you use Dropbox or Google Drive for file storage, this is a great example of Infrastructure as a Service.

The next phase, primarily pushed by PTC and Siemens-PLM, was the hosting of the PLM platform on a specific cloud partner's hardware such as NetIDEAS, IBM, or HP, running the app servers, databases, and file stores on an appliance (a server blade) which was a primitive form of Platform as a Service (PaaS). It was still operated on a single-tenant basis (dedicated hardware for each hosted customer) and allowed for some further cost reduction, but the primary issue here was the continuing massive cost of upgrades due to customization. In other words, the cost of maintaining hardware and networking had been reduced, but the software maintenance costs were still abominably high, and adoption slowed down because it was deemed easier to do everything in-house. Today, Aras Innovator is still sold in this way on the Azure store. Services providers such as Minerva PLM setup instances of Aras Innovator on AWS and manage them for their customers. These are all examples of PLM on Cloud as PaaS, not to be confused with SaaS. To take more common examples, if your company uses Salesforce.com for its sales automation or customer relationship management (CRM) processes, this is an example of leveraging the Force.com platform as a service because all software in the Salesforce suite is built on this common platform (and we will talk about a PLM product, Propel PLM, also built on this cloud-native platform.) Figures 11, 12 and 13 are shown below to help illustrate the differences between PaaS and SaaS models.

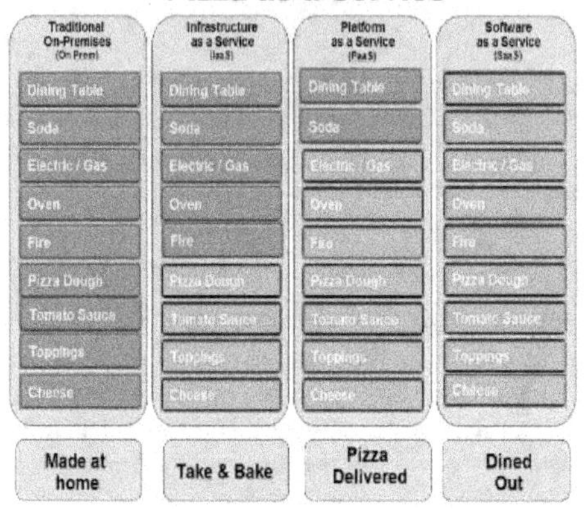

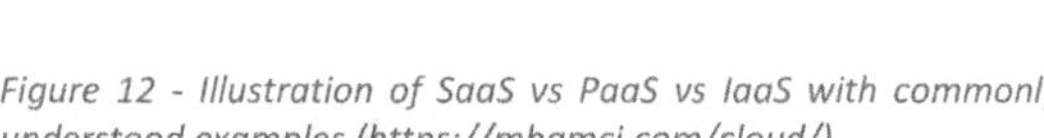

Figure 11 - Pizza as a Service https://tinyurl.com/y77wqq2s. This is a good illustration at a very high-level to explain the differences between On-Prem PLM and the increasing levels of service from IaaS to SaaS from Albert Baron of IBM in 2014.

Figure 12 - Illustration of SaaS vs PaaS vs IaaS with commonly understood examples (https://mbamci.com/cloud/)

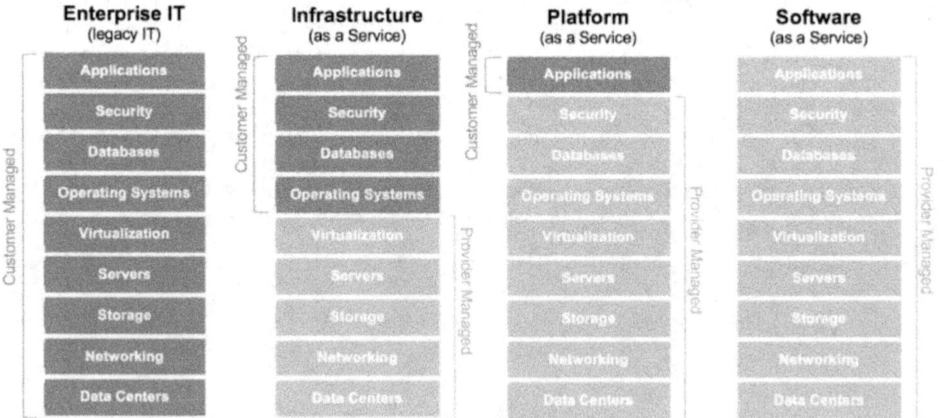

Figure 13 - Details of IaaS vs PaaS vs SaaS (https://mbamci.com/cloud/)

Each of the Billion Dollar Club vendors has released or announced new portfolios of SaaS offerings hosted at one of the major cloud vendors (primarily Amazon Web Services or Microsoft Azure) or their own cloud provider (French provider Outscale for Dassault's **3DEXPERIENCE** platform). For Dassault, Autodesk and Siemens, the default choice is AWS (in fact, for Autodesk it is the ONLY choice); for PTC and Aras, the default is Azure. We have also seen a wave of smaller, more focused SaaS-only PLM platforms such as OpenBOM, Propel PLM and Upchain. This new way of deploying PLM harkens back to the old days of mainframe computing (shared resources with unique logins) but was given the sexier name of "cloud" to make an old idea sound new. In this case, you access all the PLM functionality via a web address and pay a monthly or yearly subscription based on how many platform apps you use or how many users you connect to the platform. Some explanatory examples shown below in Table 1. For more common examples, when you used Facebook or Gmail, you are using a Software as a Service because you just consume the applications with no concerns about administering the services themselves.

Table 1 - Comparing PaaS and SaaS with Cloud PLM

COMPARING PAAS AND SAAS FOR CLOUD PLM

Non-functional Requirements	PaaS / Managed Service	SaaS / Software as a Service
Multi-Tenant	No	Yes[1]
Access to Command Line Prompt	Yes	No
Upgrade / Patch Management	Manual by Service Provider	Automated by Vendor
Degree of Customization	Normally unlimited	Vendor-dependent
Configuration Files	Sometimes	Never
VPN Access	Yes	Yes, but not always
External Integrations	Yes	Vendor-dependent

1 – Some vendors offer SaaS with mono-tenant, DS Private Cloud is one example as well as PTC Windchill.

It must be noted that the term SaaS refers to how the services are delivered and paid for, in other words that the software is paid for on a subscription/all-in model and users connect via the internet, intranet, or VPN. The servers are, however, not necessarily in the data center of a hosting partner. SAP, IBM, and other vendors offer SaaS services that are run on hardware that is in the customer's on-premises data center. The HPE Greenlake cloud services, as another example, allows for running software in the customer data center or on the cloud of the customer's choice and can move workloads to between on-premises hardware or cloud hardware transparently. And in the case that the customer wants to bring back all their data and control to their own personnel and data center, it is just a contractual change but transparent from a hardware point of view. In fact, many of the largest companies are already doing SaaS, but within their own datacenters.

Oleg Shilovitsky at Beyond PLM has written a great blog article describing SaaS and PLM[12]. First pioneered to great success in the CRM world by SalesForce, the holy grail of a customizable and upgradable system wholly dematerialized on the cloud sounds very appealing. We have already described how SaaS PLM has been pushed by each of the major PLM vendors. But how effective is it and why aren't more companies moving there? What are the advantages and disadvantages of this approach? And, no one really questions moving CRM to the cloud, why is PLM any different?

[12] http://beyondplm.com/2019/12/29/saas-plm-what-do-you-need-to-know-about-cloud-architecture-and-data-management-in-2020/

If CRM then PLM, or why is PLM different?

Let me address that last question first. Customer Relationship Management (CRM) is a totally different animal than PLM. The data used by CRM is primarily user input into forms, surveys, etc. whereas PLM deals in multiple complex external formats and files that are typically much larger than an HTML form can encapsulate. CRM is highly collaborative and relatively self-contained, particularly when we look at SalesForce which also includes basic human resources (HR), billing, and accounting pieces. There is also no physical, manufactured object (a car, a plane) behind it, whereas PLM is not only dealing in planes, trains, and automobiles but also labeling, pharmaceuticals, oil rigs, etc. and is connected to CAD and ERP systems and often other systems such as manufacturing execution (MES), master data management (MDM), maintenance, repair and operations (MRO). In other words, the data that PLM deals with is far more heterogeneous than that inside a CRM and it requires multiple external integrations to live up to its full potential.

The data that PLM manages changes at a much faster rate as well. Every modification on a design, no matter how small, by any designer or engineer makes an update to the PLM system. This can amount to tens of thousands of changes per day or more. This creates unique challenges in terms of concurrent collaboration on complex models and BOMs in terms of assuring that all users are working on the latest and greatest data. This means that PLM solutions are inherently different than the CRM systems and have very different constraints. For reasons to be discussed below, there are things that the cloud is great at which can be very helpful within PLM and other things that remain quite challenging. One notable exception to this, however, is the Propel PLM solution which was built based on SalesForce.com's development platform. It is a viable solution for smaller customers, but its product breadth and capabilities are relatively immature and limited when compared to the Billion Dollar Club and it does not have its own CAD platform. It is primarily for customers that do not have massive files to be moved around and collaborated upon, so it is not for everyone, but it leverages the power of the Force.com platform including its wide variety of integration options: Mulesoft, Zapier, Informatica, Jitterbit, and Tibco allowing their customers to leverage the strength and breadth of Salesforce while adopting and optimizing PLM.

PLM manages data that is orders of magnitude more complex than what is typically found in CRM and that data is constantly on the move. For designing a product, there is CAD data, the metadata about the models (attributes, dimensions, constraints, materials, etc.) as well as all the data pertaining to projects, change management, and the plethora of other functions that PLM provides. The data can come in different formats and is exchanged with a wide variety of other enterprise systems such as ERP and various manufacturing systems (MOM, MES, etc.) PLM platforms and CRM platforms are quite different, particularly when dealing with 3D models and simulation data, and therefore PLM deployment on the cloud has unique challenges that make it more difficult to manage. See Table 2 below for a summary of the differences between the data managed by CRM and the data managed by PLM.

COMPARING CRM AND PLM SYSTEMS

Characteristics	CRM	PLM
Data Complexity	Relatively Simple	Very Complex and Interrelated
Data Formats	Relatively Homogeneous	Very Heterogeneous
Object Relationships	Relatively Simple	Extremely Complex
Nature of System	Highly Transactional	Highly Collaborative
Use of 3D Data	Only for Advanced Analytics	Consistently Across All Processes
Data Replication	Unnecessary	Required for Remote CAD Workers
External Integrations	Mostly to HR and Point of Sales Systems	ERP, CRM, CAD, MES, IOT, etc.

One differentiator for SalesForce is its multi-tenant architecture which was part of the DNA of the Force.com since its introduction[13]. This means that in a single running application server, many customers can be hosted simultaneously without risk of customers seeing each other's data. The platform architecture must be natively cloud with no configuration files and it must allow modifying the data model for one customer without impacting any other customers, which is how Autodesk Fusion Lifecycle, Propel PLM, Arena, OpenBOM and Upchain are built. The advantage of multi-tenancy is to optimize physical hardware by reducing idle cycles and far better margins for the software vendor. In terms of data security, it is critical that the customer data is segmented and isolated from all other customers (or tenants) to prevent leakage or bleeding of information. The disadvantage for older, monolithic platforms such as **3D**EXPERIENCE and Teamcenter X is the cost of rewriting kernels and applications to respect the unique TenantID of each customer's environment in order to keep each customer's IP siloed off from the others which has led to some features being cloud-only or on-premises only.

Of the current market offerings in PLM (other than the aforementioned Propel PLM based on SalesForce), **3D**EXPERIENCE, Arena, OpenBOM, Upchain and Autodesk Fusion Lifecycle are advertised as being multi-tenant. For **3D**EXPERIENCE on DS Public Cloud, several customers will run on the same infrastructure, but as the architecture was not rewritten from the ground up to allow multitenancy, this means that the level of customization is severely restricted (discussed later in this paper). Teamcenter X's SaaS platform ("Base" and "Add-ons") are both multi-tenant and allow very limited configuration. Windchill is currently single tenant, but they have plans for a re-introducing a multi-tenant version later on, thus leveraging their new Atlas platform.

---

[13] The Force.com Multitenant Architecture: Understanding the Design of Salesforce.com's Internet Application Development Platform from SalesForce.com (10/15/2008)

<u>Am I taking a risk with respect to my Intellectual Property?</u>

I think that one of the first objections to moving product development to the cloud is the concern around the security of the invaluable Intellectual Property (IP) which is no longer safeguarded in the dark, dusty machine room. Is this a legitimate concern? Yes and no. Yes, this means that if the cloud-based PLM system is hacked, competitors lacking in integrity could steal designs and so forth. In my mind, this is potentially an issue but with low probability. First off, the dark, dusty machine room rarely has adequate security and the most common IP theft comes not from freelance hackers[14], but from disgruntled or corrupt employees shoving a USB key in the back of the server and then taking a plane out of the country. From this perspective, cloud does curtail internal piracy because there is no server in which to stick a USB key. As for external hackers, Azure, AWS, as well as Salesforce.com are all sufficiently secure to prevent all but the most persistent and clever hackers, but those hackers are most interested in the quick money to be made in identity theft, banking, and credit card data to bother with the complexities of figuring out among the terabytes of PLM data, what is truly important and what could not be exploited for financial gain. I feel that, in terms of data security, the cloud is potentially equally secure, if not more secure, if all disaster recovery, encryption, and hardening of identity management and virtual machines are implemented rigorously. See Table 3 below for a summary of the various vulnerabilities and counter-measures faced by software today.

Table 3- Comparing Vulnerabilities of Cloud vs On Premises

IS THE CLOUD MORE OR LESS SAFE THAN ON PREMISES?

Attack Type	On Prem System Vulnerable?	Cloud-based System Vulnerable?	Internal vs External Hackers	On Prem Countermeasure	Cloud Countermeasure(s) Type(s)
Distributed Denial of Service	X	X	External	Firewalls, VPNs	ISO[1] / SOC[2] / OWASP
Session Hijacking	X	X	Both	Firewalls, VPNs	ISO[1] / SOC[2] / OWASP
Drive-by Attack	X	X	External	Firewalls, VPNs	OWASP
Password Attack	X	X	External	Firewalls, VPNs	OWASP
Phishing-type Attacks	X	X	External	Firewalls, VPNs	OWASP
Physical Hack of Hardware	X		Internal	ISO[1] / SOC[2]	ISO[1] / SOC[2]

1 – ISO = ISO 27001:2013
2 – SOC = SOC 2 Type 2

There are many standards now for the security of data stored in the cloud[15]. The SOC II standard is one of the highest. Companies are required to submit to an audit by a certified auditor's review in order to verify that their datacenters are accessible by a strictly controlled number of people who have all passed background security checks. There have to be firewalls and powerful encryption methods deployed for data in flight (going over a network connection) as well as encryption for data at rest (residing on some form of storage). SaaS, PaaS and IaaS vendors such as AWS, Azure, Salesforce and Oracle typically have SOC II Type 2 certification. The ISO 27001:2013 standard is for software companies to prove that they are resistant to hacking. There is also a constantly updated list called the Open Web Application Security Project (OWASP) of the most frequent

---

[14] Note the very recent hacks at Twitter: https://www.theverge.com/2020/7/15/21326656/twitter-hack-explanation-bitcoin-accounts-employee-tools

[15] I found this site particularly useful in describing SOC II and others: https://www.itgovernance.co.uk/soc-reporting

software vulnerabilities and countermeasures that companies typically follow closely. Above and beyond these, there are the government-mandated security levels such as FEDRAMP and ITAR discussed below. For a fully secure system, customers must ensure that each level of their stack (IaaS, PaaS, and SaaS) is fully compliant with these industry standards.

What about industrial espionage from foreign powers?

There is one caveat to this argument, however. Rogue governments and governmental agencies could potentially hack into the cloud and steal data for industrial espionage. In this case, taking a cloud partner that does not leave backdoors for the CIA (AWS built the CIA cloud back in 2013/2014) and is not located in China with a history of dubious ethics (Huawei[16]) would be advisable. There are cases where foreign governments were able to add spyware chips to server hardware that was installed in "secure" AWS datacenters[17]. Of the other cloud providers, Microsoft Azure seems to be the most proactive in this regard[18]. If this issue is of overwhelming concern, then see the ITAR section later in this white paper.

While it is nearly impossible to be absolutely certain that your system is impenetrable other than by completely isolating it from any networks, there are some things that can be done as countermeasures. Ensuring that all data in transit (or "in flight") is encrypted via SSL/TLS is a basic security measure that is universally implemented in PLM systems. Beyond this, encrypting databases and the files (data "at rest") is a further method for protecting IP. Teamcenter X and PTC offer digital rights management (DRM) kinds of technologies to protect specific documents from being viewed or modified. Using secure two-phase authentication is an effective way for blocking unwanted users. Lastly, companies should always be punctilious in traceability so that if your product shows up somewhere it is not supposed to, you have a digital stamp as proof of your ownership. The company Qore8 (formerly Coastal Logic) has robust digital stamping and digital certificate management plugins for PLM.

One common concept for cloud security is called "defense in depth" according to which each server and network on which sensitive data is stored or transmitted are secured individually. It is usually referred to in three layers: Physical Controls, Technical Controls, and Administrative Controls. Some examples of defense in depth include firewalls, antivirus software, encryption, demilitarized zones (DMZ), virtual private networks (VPN), and biometrics. The best cloud companies will typically describe their efforts with regards to this security approach. Besides the big cloud providers Azure and AWS, PLM vendors such as Autodesk[19], PTC[20] and Dassault Systèmes[21] have also published detailed white papers describing their use of Defense in Depth and Arena discusses it on their website[22].

From a software development point of view, the most common vulnerabilities are regularly listed in the Open Web Application Security Project (OWASP) as well as the best countermeasures. The best cloud software providers will always reference their constant surveillance of the OWASP list and mention expedited patching

[16] https://www.wsj.com/articles/huaweis-yearslong-rise-is-littered-with-accusations-of-theft-and-dubious-ethics-11558756858

[17] https://www.bloomberg.com/news/features/2018-10-04/the-big-hack-how-china-used-a-tiny-chip-to-infiltrate-america-s-top-companies

[18] https://azure.microsoft.com/en-us/overview/azure-ip-advantage/

[19] https://www.autodeskfusionlifecycle.com/app/uploads/2020/02/security-whitepaper.pdf

[20] https://www.ptc.com/-/media/Files/PDFs/Services/Cloud-Security-Whitepaper.pdf

[21] https://www.3ds.com/products-services/3dexperience/resources/whitepapers/cloud-security/ [Caveat emptor: I wrote this particular white paper.]

[22] https://www.arenasolutions.com/security-platform/

for any vulnerabilities that are discovered between major releases. Table 4 lists the various PLM platforms along with the implementation of security standards and counter-measures.

Table 4 - SaaS PLM Security and Countermeasures

SAAS PLM SECURITY AND COUNTERMEASURES

Vendor	Solution	Data Encryption In Flight	SSL/TLS Web Connect	Data Encryption At Rest	DRM Solution option for PLM Documents	SAML-based SSO w/two-factor Authentication	Redundant Data Centers for Disaster Recovery	Security in Depth	OWASP
Dassault[1]	**3D**EXPERIENCE	Yes	Yes	No	No	Yes	Yes	Yes	Yes
PTC[2]	Windchill	Yes	Yes	Optional	Yes	Yes	Yes	Yes	Yes
Siemens	Teamcenter	Yes	Yes	Yes	Yes	Yes	Yes	Yes	Yes
Autodesk[4]	Fusion Lifecycle	Yes	Yes	No	No	Yes	Yes	Yes	Yes
Aras	Innovator	Yes	Yes	Customer-dependent	Customer-dependent	Customer-dependent	Customer-dependent	Customer-dependent	Yes
Arena[5]	Arena	Yes	Yes	Yes	No	Yes	Yes	Yes	Yes
OpenBOM	OpenBOM	Yes	Yes	Yes	No	Yes[6]	Yes	Yes	Yes
Oracle	PLM Cloud	Yes	Yes	Optional	Yes	Yes	Yes	Yes	Yes
Propel	Propel PLM	Yes	Yes	Yes[7]	No	Yes	Yes	Yes	Yes
Upchain	Upchain	Yes	Yes	Yes	No	No[8]	Yes	Yes	Yes

1 - https://www.3ds.com/products-services/3dexperience/resources/whitepapers/cloud-security/
2 - https://www.ptc.com/-/media/Files/PDFs/Services/Cloud-Security-Whitepaper.pdf
3 – Teamcenter leverages the S3 based DSS service where data is encrypted by default (provided by AWS). The database is not encrypted, but it is inaccessible from outside their cloud environment (VPC)
4 - https://www.autodeskfusionlifecycle.com/app/uploads/2020/02/security-whitepaper.pdf
5 - https://www.arenasolutions.com/platform/infrastructure/
6 – Optional for Enterprise Subscribers
7 – Available with Shield option from Salesforce.com
8 – Upchain SAML support coming 1Q21

What if I have FEDRAMP or ITAR requirements?

For industries that are manipulate government-sensitive data, higher levels of security and access are imposed by regulatory and governmental authorities. There are questions of the security of the data center itself which, in the United States, are bound up in the various levels of Federal Risk and Authorization Management Program (FEDRAMP) security standard, released in 2012. The US Department of Defense created even stricter controls for military assets and intellectual property (IP), the highest standard being Impact Level 5 (IL5). Applications also have to demonstrate that they can prevent users from accessing data depending on the nationality of the user and the physical location (the country in particular) from which they are accessing the system on the cloud. The International Traffic in Arms Regulations (ITAR) and the Export Administration Regulations (EAR) are two important United States export control laws that affect the manufacturing, sales and distribution of technology and must be implemented by software vendors in their login and authentication processes. ITAR and FEDRAMP compliance can be two major showstoppers in competing for contracts particularly in the aerospace and defense industry.

Most of the PaaS vendors will allow hosting on FEDRAMP-compliant clouds such as AWS Government Cloud, but as this is just on-premises computing moved to a secure cloud, the management of the system can be contained within the US, because it is critical for ITAR that no foreign employee can access the systems. SaaS systems, on the other hand, which have central management for patching must be able to prove that all management is done by US nationals on US soil. The DS Public Cloud requires R&D intervention from France and India for patch and upgrade management and therefore does not qualify for FEDRAMP or ITAR. The DS Private Cloud has similar constraints, so for **3D**EXPERIENCE, the only option is to use a PaaS and find a US-based service provider. For the other two of the Billion Dollar Club, Siemens talks about several available security levels for their Siemens

Security Stack including ITAR and FEDRAMP on AWS, and PTC advertises compatibility with FEDRAMP-compliant clouds on their webpages. PTC also has the illustrious IL5 certification, one of the highest security levels available for working with the US military. Arena Solutions also touts a FEDRAMP-compatible cloud whereas Aras Innovator does not mention one on their website, but they have customers that are using the software on a FEDRAMP cloud and have ITAR compliance as well. Autodesk for the moment does not support FEDRAMP and has no ITAR implementation in the Fusion Lifecycle products.

Another government-imposed constraint in some industries is FDA certification via auditing software implementations that touch on medical equipment in order to guarantee that standards of quality and traceability are met.[23] So PLM vendors wanting to sell to these companies need to demonstrate that their software has robust electronic signature management, an integrated Corrective Action and Preventive Action workflow, Device Master Record (DMR) management, and many other specifics required by the FDA to ensure the security of products related to food, medicine, and medical devices.

The following Table 5 shows some common CFR requirements that the Teamcenter X team has implemented for their Medical Devices customers in Teamcenter (on-premise) and are either inherently available in Teamcenter X or can be easily configured. This is not an exhaustive list and each vendor will have a similar list if they work in this industry.

Table 5 - CFR Requirements for Medical Devices Implemented in Teamcenter

CFR part 11: The system shall provide a secure, computer-generated, time-stamped audit trail
CFR part 11: The audit trail shall independently record the date and time of operator entries and actions that create, modify or delete electronic records.
CFR part 11: The audit trail shall ensure record changes do not obscure previously recorded information.
CFR part 11: The audit trail information is retained for a period minimally in accordance with the companies record retention policy. CareFusion will never delete the audit trails.
CFR part 11: The system shall ensure the audit trail information is available for regulatory agency review through the use of application screens, system reports and queries.
CFR part 11: The system shall record the time in the audit trail in GMT.
CFR part 11: The system shall record changes to metadata properties that occur on a given object when it is revised.
CFR part 11: Electronic signatures shall employ at least two distinct identification components such as an identification code and password.
CFR part 11: Electronic Signatures will be captured when the user enters their credentials when prompted for a signature.
CFR part 11: The system shall store the approver's ID, decision, and approval date and time when the user provides their electronic approval.
CFR part 11: The system shall provide the capability to prompt for user credentials before providing access to the system.

---

[23] Good white paper from Siemens Teamcenter here: https://www.plm.automation.siemens.com/en_us/Images/11866_tcm1023-47162.pdf

Please note that FEDRAMP systems are all very expensive and will easily exceed the cost of on-premises solutions due to the additional security and data redundancy required. Customers need to modify their default environment to adapt to conform to FDA requirements. See Table 6 below for a summary of FEDRAMP/ITAR Support for the primary PLM vendors.

Table 6 - FEDRAMP/ITAR Support for Major PLM Vendors

FEDRAMP/ITAR SUPPORT

Vendor	Solution	FEDRAMP	ITAR	SOC II Type 2	ISO 27001:2013	Implements Features Req'd for FDA Certification
Dassault Systèmes	**3D**EXPERIENCE	No	Yes[1]	Yes	Yes	On Premises only
PTC	Windchill	Yes	Yes	Yes	Yes	Yes
Siemens	Teamcenter	No[2]	Yes	Yes	Yes	Yes
Autodesk	Fusion Lifecycle	No	No	Yes	Yes	Yes
Aras	Aras Innovator	Yes	Yes	Yes	Yes	Yes
Arena	Arena	Yes	Yes	Yes	Yes	Yes
OpenBOM	OpenBOM	No	No	No[3]	No[3]	No
Oracle	PLM Cloud	Yes	Yes	Yes	Yes	Yes
Propel	Propel PLM	Yes	Yes	Yes	Yes	Yes
Upchain	Upchain	No	Yes	No[4]	Yes	No

1 - ITAR option available on-premises or DS Private Cloud only   2 – FEDRAMP certification ongoing. Expected in early 2021
3 – SOC 2 Type II and ISO 27001:2013 expected for OpenBOM in 1Q21.   4 – Upchain is already SOC II Type 1. Soc II Type 2 coming in 1Q21

Is Cloud cheaper for PLM in the long run?

Perhaps a more meaningful concern is whether the cloud-based SaaS platforms will truly improve time to market and profitability. Certainly, in the short run, moving from annual license cost (ALC) and perpetual license cost (PLC) to a subscription-based model (QLC or YLC) with support nominally included does save money. Despite the higher cost of SaaS and PaaS (because there is typically a roughly 20% or more uplift in price to cover the infrastructure that is included with the software), since there is no initial outlay for expensive hardware, the economics are weighed heavily in favor of SaaS (or PaaS). However, after three years or so, the cost of cloud-based SaaS which is more or less linear and flat will exceed the ALC/PLC cost (which is spent upfront and depreciated), so more benefit needs to be derived from the solutions themselves for the switch to make sense financially. If the system has not started to make major improvements to how the company designs and builds their products in the first two years of deployment, then ultimately, the entire project becomes risky since the cost outweighs the benefits, and it is likely that management could withdraw support of the effort. See Figures 14 and 15 for some examples and slide 21 for a summary of the pricing strategy for the major Cloud PLM vendors.

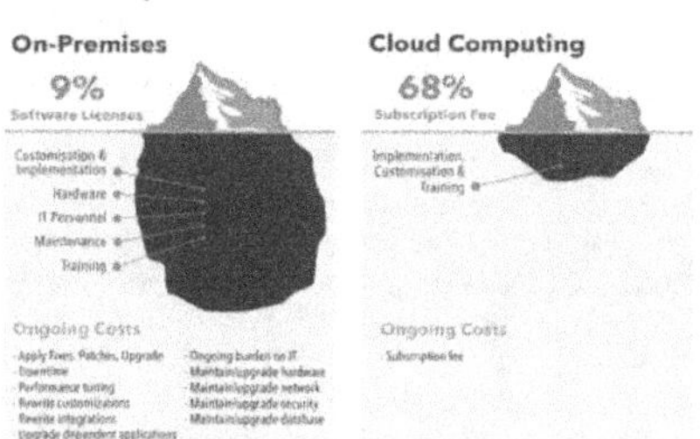

Figure 14 - Iceberg analogy for Cloud vs On-Premises Cost (Source: https://www.jedox.com/en/blog/keep-your-head-in-the-cloud-and-feet-on-the-ground-when-choosing-your-cpm-solution/)

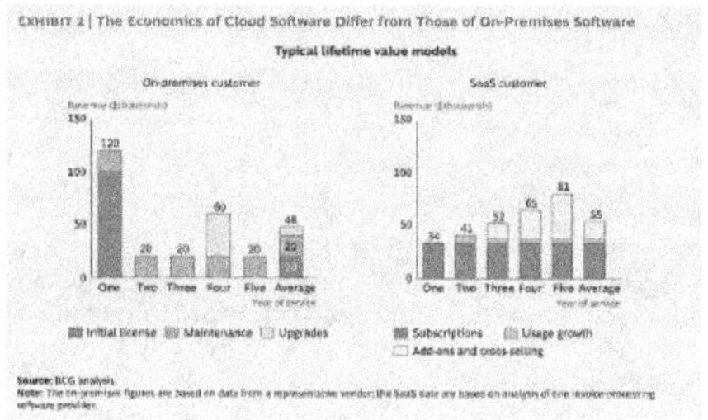

Figure 15 - Relative costs over five years for On-premises and SaaS – cloud is not always cheaper, just different (Source: https://www.silicon.fr/hub/hpe-intel-hub/serveurs-et-stockage-externaliser-est-il-synonyme-deconomies)

Another interesting aspect here is the interest of the PLM vendor to go to a SaaS platform. If we look at the margins that companies make just from implementation services, it runs at about 30% overall because of the heavy human overhead involved. When a company moves to SaaS, that margin jumps to about 70-80% due to the mutualization of hardware and automation of the sales process. Some of this benefit is derived from the savings in deployment time, as cloud infrastructures are deployable in a small fraction of time compared to on-premises software. Typically, the newer software is also easier to use and thus the learning curve for employees is less steep. Another benefit, particularly when talking of SaaS offers, is the time to value because the software is already nearly ready to use as is. This begs the question of how adaptable is the software to my business environment?

Another key aspect to looking at the return on investment (ROI) for adopting a SaaS strategy with PLM is the savings for migrations and upgrades. I'll cover this in more detail later in this white paper, but the weeks and months of aggravation that are usually consumed when upgrading an On-Premises PLM system have typically been daunting at best. Most SaaS vendors include the upgrades transparently in their pricing, so the fact that this is no longer a risk in terms of missing deployment dates due to unforeseen upgrade or patching issues, this factor needs to be taken into account when looking at the overall cost of the deployment. See Table 7 below for a summary of PLM vendor pricing.

Table 7 - SaaS PLM Pricing Summary

SAAS PLM PRICING

Vendor	Platform	User-based or Server-based pricing	Public Price List?	Price Tiers (if Applicable)	Free Trial Version?
Dassault	3DEXPERIENCE	Named User Pricing	Not Public	From $37.50/user/month[1]	No
Siemens	Teamcenter X	Named User Pricing	Not Public	N/A	Yes
PTC	Windchill	Server Pricing	Not Public	N/A	No
Autodesk	Fusion Lifecycle	Named User Pricing	Public	User/Yearly: $325-$965-$1935[2]	Yes[3]
Aras	Innovator	Add-ons and Consulting Support	Public	Starts at $79/User/Month for >250 users for upgrades, etc[4]	Yes
Arena	Arena	Named User Pricing	Not Public	N/A	Yes
OpenBOM	OpenBOM	Named User, Team, and Company Pricing	Public	Monthly: $25/user-$125/team-$375/company[5]	Yes
Oracle	PLM Cloud	Named User Pricing	Public	$500/user/month (minimum 10 users)[6]	No
Propel	Propel PLM	Named User Pricing	Public	User/Yearly: $1000-$1500-$2200[7]	Yes
Upchain	Upchain	Named User Pricing	Public	User/Monthly: $30-$70-$200[8]	Yes

1 – For minimum Collaborative Business Innovator. Startup offer exists at $474/user/year: https://www.3ds.com/3dexperience/cloud/startups
2 - At Enterprise Tier, customers get unlimited integrations and unlimited suppliers (https://www.autodeskfusionlifecycle.com/en/plm-software-pricing)
3 – https://www.autodeskfusionlifecycle.com/en/contact/plm-free-software-trial/
4 – See https://www.aras.com/en-services/subscription-pricing   5 - For $375/year, customers get unlimited users, unlimited integrations: https://www.openbom.com/pricing
6 - https://www.oracle.com/applications/supply-chain-management/product-lifecycle-management/
7 - https://www.propelplm.com/products/how-to-buy   8 - https://www.upchain.com/pricing/

Do I have to compromise on functionality if I go to Cloud?

Ultimately, the most important consideration is whether the cloud-based PLM system is functionally superior to the on-premise system. Is the entire on-premise portfolio available on the cloud or are there significant pieces of the puzzle that are still only available on-premises? Speaking from my experience at Dassault, this continues to be a key inhibitor to success with DS cloud and I suspect that the other platforms have similar issues (although I would be pleased to be proven wrong in the comments on this article). Despite more and more of the DS portfolio being made available on the cloud, there are still many apps and processes (DS terminology for the ENOVIA, CATIA, DELMIA, SIMULIA, and BIOVIA applications that run on top of the cloud-based **3D**EXPERIENCE platform) that are still available only on the on-premises portfolio. To make things more appetizing for customers to adopt DS Public Cloud, there are DS apps that are exclusively cloud-only, such as the Process Planner (XPP) or 3DDrive. But, as one dives deeper into the technology, one finds significant gaps in the connections between engineering bill of materials (EBOM) and manufacturing bill of materials (MBOM) and a confusion of apps using older and newer (and incompatible) data models[24] which makes it challenging, if not impossible, to implement a full cradle-to-grave PLM process.

For Siemens and their Teamcenter X platform, the SaaS offerings, called "Base" and "Addons" are both pared-down parts of the portfolio operated in multi-tenant mode. When you move to "Personalized", you are actually using the full Teamcenter portfolio in a managed service in a mono-tenant PaaS rather than in multi-tenant SaaS mode but connected to the multi-tenant "Base" system transparently. The full platform is, of course, also available on-premises. Mendix is the scripting engine used for much of the process-based modeling.

PTC offers Windchill as a SaaS, but in mono-tenant mode as well as the identical portfolio as managed services/PaaS or on-premises. Each of the deployments offers the same integration via microservices to other

---

[24] https://www.linkedin.com/pulse/demystifying-powerby-3dexperience-michael-finocchiaro

systems. Customization can be done via the standard Windchill tools without restriction. However, PTC allows moving data from the SaaS offer to the PaaS offer, but the price will vary depending on how much customization was made. The forthcoming Atlas platform will add a multi-tenant SaaS mode to this range of solutions in the future.

For Aras Innovator, the product is identical whether on-premises or as a PaaS solution. As for Upchain, Autodesk Fusion Lifecycle, OpenBOM and other multi-tenant SaaS platforms, they are only available on cloud, so the question does not really apply. See Table 8 for more details.

Table 8 - Multi-tenancy and Cloud Portfolios for PLM Vendors

MULTI-TENANT AND CLOUD CHOICES

Vendor	SaaS Offering	SaaS is Multi-tenant?	PaaS Offering	On Premises
Dassault Systèmes	3DEXPERIENCE DS Public Cloud Portfolio[1]	Yes	Only from 3rd Parties (Technia.Cloud, etc)	3DEXPERIENCE On Premises Portfolio
PTC	Windchill Full Portfolio	No[2]	Windchill Full Portfolio and 3rd Party Hosting	Windchill Full Portfolio
Siemens	Teamcenter X Base and Addons (multi-tenant) Personalized (mono-tenant)	Yes	Teamcenter X Full Portfolio and 3rd Party Hosting	Teamcenter X Full Portfolio
Autodesk	Fusion Lifecycle	Yes	N/A	Autodesk Vault
Aras	N/A	N/A	Yes	Aras Innovator
Arena	Full Portfolio	Yes	N/A	N/A
OpenBOM	Full Portfolio	Yes	N/A	N/A
Oracle	Product Lifecycle Management Product Hub	Yes	Oracle Private Cloud	Oracle Agile
Propel PLM	Full Portfolio	Yes	N/A	N/A
Upchain	Full Portfolio	Yes	N/A	N/A

Notes:
1 - DS Private Cloud also available in SaaS, but it is single tenant with a VPN. It has nearly an identical portfolio to that of DS Public Cloud
2 – Forthcoming PTC Atlas platform will be multi-tenant and current Vuforia AR/VR backend is already multi-tenant

Can I get my data into and out of the cloud as my business needs change?

Another major inhibitor is the lack of turnkey tools to migrate data from on-premises to cloud-based platforms, meaning that migration to and from cloud remains a major issue. This means that cloud-minded customers are forced to reduce the scope of their project to cover only engineering or manufacturing and fight the arduous battle of data movement between cloud and on-premise systems to safeguard the continuity of their digital thread. For startups who are primarily interested in design and EBOM, or for contract manufacturers focused only on the MBOM, this might not be a showstopper, but for companies that wish to own their digital twins end-to-end, it is often easier to explore IaaS or PaaS or stick to on-premises rather than take the risk of not meeting deadlines due to functional gaps.

Similarly, the issue of vendor lock-in is a legitimate concern. Unless it is explicit in the contracts signed with the cloud PLM vendor, there could be potential issues removing IP from one PLM cloud solution and moving back on-premises or to a competitive solution. On-premises, the data is right there in the hard drives, so given some sweat and muscle, the data can be extracted from a legacy system and moved elsewhere. However, since the cloud data is by definition "out there", customers need to ensure that should it be required for whatever reason to move the data out of a PLM Cloud, that they will be able to do so physically with access to the databases and file stores in the cloud and without involving Legal in the fight to get their data back.

Siemens, PTC, Autodesk, and Aras all claim that they will allow a customer to extract their data if so desired. Both Siemens and PTC also allow "lift and shift" methods for moving environments from the SaaS environment to the PaaS environment and the mechanisms are already in place. In the case of Dassault, CATIA data can be extracted via 3DXML export and some project data to Microsoft Project, but much of the ENOVIA data is not movable. DS does not provide their own PaaS environment, nor can they migrate a customer from SaaS to on-premises. Table 9 summarizes my findings concerning Vendor Lock-In.

Table 9 - SaaS PLM Vendor Lock-In

SAAS PLM VENDOR LOCK-IN

Vendor	Platform	Transfer to PaaS	Transfer to On Prem	Export all data
Dassault	3DEXPERIENCE	N/A	No	Partial
Siemens	Teamcenter X	Yes	Yes (fees apply)	Yes
PTC	Windchill	Yes (fees apply)	Yes (fees apply)	Yes
Autodesk	Fusion Lifecycle	N/A	No On-Prem Version	Yes
Aras	Innovator	N/A	Yes	Yes
Arena	Arena	N/A	No On-Prem Version	Yes
OpenBOM	OpenBOM	N/A	No On-Prem Version	Yes
Oracle	PLM Cloud	Yes (fees apply)	No On-Prem Version	Yes
Propel	Propel PLM	N/A	No On-Prem Version	Yes
Upchain	Upchain	N/A	No On-Prem Version	Yes

One thing not to lose sight of in the cloud discussion is the very real danger of a disruptive event, whether it be political, seismic, a fire, or financial that would require repatriating all of the data stored on the cloud back on premises. If the company has already sold off their data center and hardware as well as shed its remaining IT employees, how will that transition back to a data center work? The cost would be astronomically expensive to, in panic mode, rehire IT expertise, rebuild a data center and then get all the systems and data accessible to engineers and factories again. For that reason, hybrid solutions which retain some hardware and skills on site, or at a strict minimum in a co-hosting data center, would seem to be a wise approach. To take and extreme example, during the Fukushima disaster in Japan which occurred on 11 March 2011, many of the controls for the reactors were in the Fukushima Off-Site Center in Ookuma and it took three days to regain control of the remaining emergency systems which was established on 14 March 2011[25]. Had the controls been local rather than off-site, some of the massive damage may have been forestalled. The point here is that the idea of a fully 100% on cloud enterprise is a dangerous myth and that the only way it can work is via a hybrid architecture. There are gains to be made by moving towards cloud as an economic model and as a user experience, but the very real possibility of an unplanned catastrophe should never be ignored and plans should be in place in case one occurs.

---

[25] https://www.jaea.go.jp/04/shien/en/fukushima.html

Can I still adapt the SaaS-based PLM to my business needs?

I touched on the configuration versus customization in a previous article[26] which has always been a concern with all PLM platforms. Customization of an application that is not specifically designed for the cloud will nearly always result in major issues when attempting to upgrade in the future. This is because the underlying data models become incompatible due to the modifications and this means that many man-months can be spent attempting to migrate customized data into the new system at high cost and frustration. It is important to note that due to the complexities of product development and the infinite variety of ways in which companies work and collaborate, there is, for all practical purposes, no way to deploy a fully out-of-the-box PLM and thus customization is a necessary evil in nearly all deployments.

Truly SaaS-based PLM theoretically eliminates this by restricting customization to changes which do not fundamentally modify the underlying data model, usually called "configuration" to avoid the stigma of the term "customization." One can surmise that this implies a complete rearchitecting of the PLM platform to guarantee a maximum of flexibility in modifying pieces and parts of the system without compromising the system integrity and endangering future upgrades. See Figure 16 below for an example demonstrating the cost of customization on multi-tenant systems and Figure 17 which shows some of the differences between true SaaS software and On-Premises software.

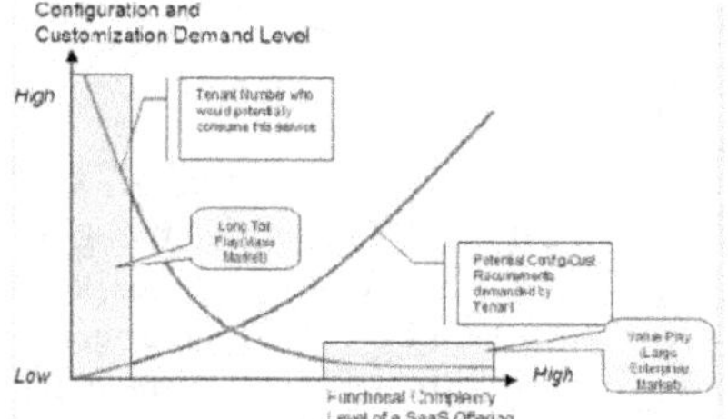

Figure 16 - Configuration vs Cost from Software as a Service: Configuration and Customization Perspectives by Wei Sun, Xin Zhang, et. al.

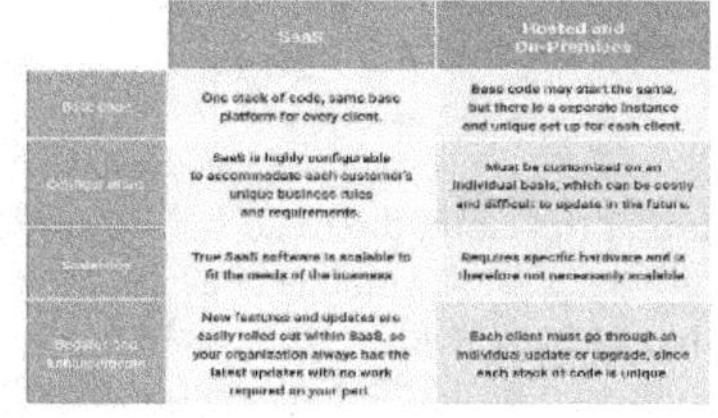

Figure 17 - Differences between SaaS and On-Premises Software paradigms (Source: https://blog.invoicecloud.net/what-is-cloudwashing-identify-true-saas-solution)

For Dassault customers in particular, this has been a painful journey which has not been completely realized as there are still many useful programming tools (triggers, Java Procedure Objects or JPOs, etc.) that are only available on a command-line and thus not accessible from the cloud. This severely limits what object behaviors can be modeled on the system. Beyond this, the issue of connecting internal and external systems with which PLM data is exchanged is also a major issue. **Without an open micro-services platform for data exchange, manufacturing data from enterprise resource planning (ERP) systems such as SAP cannot be synced with the engineering data and thus the digital thread gets cut.** Similarly, if the customer (not to mention their supply chain) is using a variety of CAD systems to design, all these systems need to be easily integrated over the cloud and this is also not always the case. Once again, either the scope of the project needs to be reduced, or it is just simpler to abandon the cloud and stick with the devil you know on-premises.

---

[26] https://www.linkedin.com/pulse/demystifying-3dexperience-customization-model-michael-finocchiaro

The one clear advantage of cloud, however, is the elimination of costly upgrade processes as in a true cloud-based SaaS PLM system, this burden is borne solely by the PLM provider. If you can accept the limitations that I mentioned above, and I know that it is possible in many cases, then you stand to save potentially years of time by eliminating painful upgrades from your PLM roadmap once cloud is adopted. I would be remiss at this point not to mention Aras Innovator as a viable PaaS-compatible platform that seems to have at least partially resolved the customization issue as I have written about on LinkedIn[27] and this has been a convincing argument for even large customers like GE Renewables to switch from one of the billion dollar platforms to Aras.

Autodesk Fusion Lifecycle is perhaps the most advanced in this aspect for multi-tenant, SaaS PLM offerings. You can create unlimited new custom objects (they are called "workspaces") and anything that is loaded into the system is fully customizable by default including objects, attributes, revision, lifecycles, workflow engine, and triggers. Most configuration is done via drag and drop in the user interface. There is also a scripting engine that allows you to write custom actions that trigger on workflow events or edits of the records, etc.

Propel PLM also has the ability to have unlimited configuration (both drag and drop and APEX code) while the ability to upgrade to every new revision in minutes or hours is one of their core differentiators from the traditional PLM vendors. Propel uses the Force.com platform and Salesforce configuration tools which allow Propel customers to draw from 100,000s of Salesforce experts and certified administrators around the world.

Similarly, Aras Innovator also offers customization without compromising updates and upgrades by upgrading the Unified Data Model, the Modeling Engine, and the Platform Services all together and allowing for customizations to be made exclusively by services outside this set of core services. It is, however, for the moment, a PaaS solution, but there are plans to move to a multi-tenant SaaS solution in the future.

The amount of customization required depends on many factors: the complexity of the object(s), the maturity of the company in designing products, the degree of digital continuity already in place, etc. A green-field (new from scratch) deployment will likely have less customization (and no painful data migration) as opposed to a brown-field (replacing an existing system) deployment[28] because there will be fewer existing processes to implement and fewer object types and attributes to create. It is important in any case to have good code governance and an agile code practice with appropriate DevOps tools in order to ensure success in any deployment with any degree of customization whether the target deployment is on-premises or on cloud.

---

[27] https://www.linkedin.com/pulse/demystifying-aras-innovator-zen-art-plm-customization-finocchiaro/
[28] See Lionel Gréalou's excellent article in Engineering.com: https://www.engineering.com/PLMERP/ArticleID/20353/Greenfield-vs-Brownfield-PLM-Implementations.aspx

Table 10 - SaaS PLM Configuration vs Customization

SAAS PLM VENDOR CUSTOMIZATION VS CONFIGURATION

Vendor	Platform	Customized Objects	Customized Attributes	Customized Workflow	Customized User Interface	Scripting Language
Dassault	**3D**EXPERIENCE	No[1]	Partial[1]	Partial[2]	Yes, via 3DDashboard widgets	EKL[3] Some Public REST APIs
Siemens	Teamcenter X	Yes	Yes	Yes	Yes, via Active Workspace	Mendix Public REST APIs
PTC	Windchill	Yes	Yes	Yes	Yes, via ThingWorx Navigator ThingWorx Flow	Public REST APIs
Autodesk	Fusion Lifecycle	Yes	Yes	Yes	Yes	Autodesk Forge Public REST APIs
Arena	Arena	Yes	Yes	Yes	Yes, via Scribe	Public REST APIs
Aras	Aras Innovator	Yes	Yes	Yes	Yes	Public REST APIs
OpenBOM	OpenBOM	Yes	Yes	Yes	Yes	Public REST APIs
Oracle	PLM Cloud	Yes	Yes	Yes	Yes	Public REST APIs
Propel	Propel PLM	Yes	Yes	Process Builder	Yes, via Flows, Drag & Drop	Apex Public REST APIs
Upchain	Upchain	Yes	Yes	Yes	Yes	Public REST APIs

1 – Collaborative Spaces Configuration Center allows for attribute assignments to a limited list of objects (primarily CATIA, DELMIA, and 3DXCITE objects). For Unified Typing (TXO) allows for deriving new objects and extending objects with new attributes, but it is not yet available on DS Private Cloud and is unlikely to be released on DS Public Cloud
3 – Only Routes are available on cloud. Triggers and Java Program Objects (JPOs) only available On Premises
4 – EKL available in CATIA rich client only

Will Cloud remove the headache of upgrades and migration?

Upgrades and patching have always been the most time-consuming and risky aspects of PLM deployments and one where cloud computing tends to offer some clear advantages. In the DS universe, the DS Public Cloud eliminates the cost and time associated with this because DS R&D manages all patching and upgrades transparently. This is a huge time-saver, but there are some potentially catastrophic drawbacks. For example, it is DS that decides when a release is made generally available (GA) and after that date, no previous version is available any longer. This can be problematic in industries, such as pharmaceutical, where each version of a software needs to be signed off by a regulatory agency such as the FDA. For the Teamcenter X SaaS offerings ("Base" and "Add-ons"), Siemens will also manage all patching and upgrades centrally.

Some **3D**EXPERIENCE PaaS vendors, such as Technia.Cloud[29] shown in Figure 18 below, offer upgrade services with their cloud platform, but these come with the same restrictions mentioned in the previous paragraph as to how much customization the customer can make on their system. Further, Technia and other companies have spent literally millions of dollars and months of time to try to dissect the complex DS upgrade process to automate it using DevOps tools such as Jira from Atlassian. There are a few huge DS customers I am aware of that are investing in using tools and technologies such as containers, Kerberos and Ansible to try to cloudify their in-house deployment of **3D**EXPERIENCE, but this requires an army of highly qualified IT people as well as direct involvement from DS R&D and Global Services. In other words, kids don't try this at home. It is advisable to stick with your current on-premises processes or move to the cloud (given the caveats in this article) or leverage the tools available from vendors like Technia (however, they are not cheap) rather than attempt to do this on your own.

---

[29] See Technia.Cloud for more information.

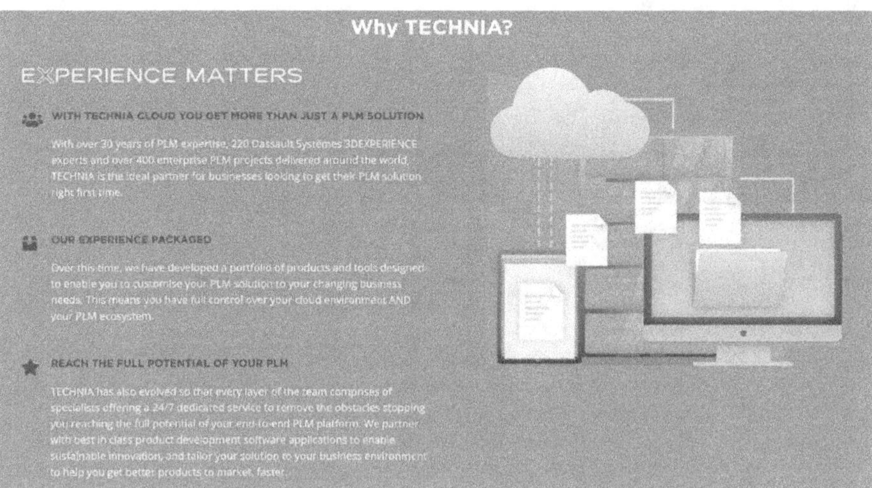

Figure 18 - Some Strong Points for Technia.Cloud hosting of 3DEXPERIENCE (https://technia.cloud/en/#solutions)

PTC has long made Windchill cloud-ready with support of containers and Kubernetes (two very fundamental technologies for managing application servers on the cloud). PaaS vendor partners such as IBM sell managed services for deploying Windchill. Based on the PTC Atlas announcements, that platform will likely follow the centrally managed upgrade/patching paradigm like those mentioned above.

Aras has always touted their ability to allow profound customization without compromising upgrades or patching, and this remains one of their primary selling points. And as it is PaaS, the customer can choose when they wish to upgrade.

The pure SaaS, multi-tenant solutions such as Autodesk Fusion Lifecycle, OpenBOM, Propel PLM and Upchain were all designed to manage patching and upgrades transparently to the user. Like other SaaS providers, Autodesk Fusion Lifecycle platform maintains all customers at the same level of the software. However, their Enterprise tier includes a sandbox with early release previews for integration testing.[30] Propel PLM releases about 30 days after the three major Salesforce.com releases and customers can opt out of the upgrades if needed. They can also get a sandbox for integration testing. Upchain releases approximately every 6-8 weeks and customers here also have a sandbox (free at the Enterprise pricing tier) and can temporarily opt out of upgrades.

---

[30] https://www.autodeskfusionlifecycle.com/en/plm-software-pricing/

CLOUD PLM VERSIONS AND UPGRADES

Vendor	Platform	Current Release Number (Aug '20)	Major Release Cycle	Interim Release Cycle	Sandbox?	Opt Out Option for Upgrades?
Dassault	**3D**EXPERIENCE	R2021x FD01	One per year	Every 8-10 weeks	Yes[1]	No
Siemens	Teamcenter X	13	Twice per year	Every 6-8 weeks	Yes[2]	No
PTC	Windchill	12.3	One per year	Every 6-8 weeks	Yes	Yes
Autodesk	Fusion Lifecycle	N/A[3]	N/A[3]	Every 6-8 weeks	Yes	No
Aras	Innovator	12.0	N/A	Every 6-8 weeks	No	Yes
Arena	Arena	2020	N/A	Every 6-8 weeks	Yes	No
OpenBOM	OpenBOM	2020	N/A	Every 4-6 weeks	No	Only at Enterprise Tier
Oracle	PLM Cloud	20C	N/A	Quarterly	Yes	No
Propel	Propel PLM	4.6	3 per year	Every 4-6 weeks	Yes[4]	Yes
Upchain	Upchain	5.4	N/A	Every 6-8 weeks	Yes[5]	Yes

1 – Public Beta environment available on request as well as commercial sandbox for 2nd non-production environment
2 - Teamcenter X customers get access to a UAT (user acceptance environment). Siemens will make the environment ready and give it to customers for testing before production and based on their feedback will fix gaps, etc.
3 – Fusion Lifecycle is on a continuous integration/development (CI/CD) program with no official release number
4 – One free sandbox and additional possible with Enterprise tier pricing
5 – At additional cost

Will Cloud fix all my PLM networking issues?

Some other overlooked issues with cloud are around networking. How will large files be passed around? What if the network is cut? These are both non-trivial and very real issues with cloud computing, but with on-premises PLM as well. PLM has long adopted various strategies for moving files closer to users via file collaboration servers (the DS term, but the other vendors have similar technologies) on-premises, but often the cloud-based solutions assume that once the data is on the cloud the problem is solved. For assemblies of several hundred parts, this is not going to work if the distributed teams are on different continents as the download times for getting the latest models will be prohibitive and frustrating for the engineers watching spinning beach balls or rotating sand-clocks for hours.

For DS Public Cloud, it is possible to replicate the entire file content into a separate data center on another continent, but if the data reaches into the terabyte range, will that really work? I am fairly sure that it is as yet an unproven process. I felt that the best approach I read about was using Autodesk Vault for local file management connected to Fusion Lifecycle on the cloud for all the collaboration tools. This approach, however, has not been widely adopted by other PLM vendors as far as I know other than Oracle Agile PLM which can be run onsite and be synched to Oracle's Product Development Cloud[31]. As for the offline aspect, there has not been enough work by PLM vendors to leverage the local data storage capabilities of HTML5 to truly work offline.

For users that are on the same campus as the hosted platform, this is not an issue of course. And for a distributed system across multiple countries, potentially cloud would potentially decrease the probability of network cuts. **Regardless, if there is no network connectivity, there is no collaboration as a rule**. With **3D**EXPERIENCE, rich clients such as CATIA will continue to work, but any features such as Lock/Unlock that require server access will not work. DS does offer an offline service, but this only works for planned downtimes,

---

[31] https://docs.oracle.com/cd/E91823_38/otn/docset.html

not random network glitches. When a cloud vendor such as AWS claims 99.9% availability, they are not considering all the switches, hubs, routers, and repeaters between your laptop and their cloud data center. The point here is that for file management and network connectivity, cloud is not the end-all-be-all of solutions and it is not highly differentiated in these areas from on-premises PLM.

That being said, if the system is designed to work in a high-latency environment, it would be able to work using WiFi or 4G networks via a laptop or portable phone in extremis. Onshape can load large assemblies even over an airplane's WiFi according to one highly placed source at PTC. So, perhaps it is an issue more limited to engineers tied down to wired corporate networks and deskside PCs and for software that is less resilient to network glitches.

The operations that are most sensitive to network connectivity and performance are those which connect to external systems: MCAD software, ECAD software and ERP packages to name the most critical. Most of the vendors offer some form of robust integrations to at least some of the market-leading software in each of the categories. See Table 12 below for a summary.

Table 12 - Cloud PLM External Integrations

SAAS PLM INTEGRATIONS

Vendor	Platform	MCAD Integrations on SaaS Platform	ECAD Integrations on SaaS Platform	ERP Integrations on SaaS Platform	Public REST APIs
Dassault	3DEXPERIENCE	POWER'BY CATIA V5, SOLIDWORKS, Draftsight, AutoCAD, Inventor, NX, SolidEdge, Creo Parametric	POWER'BY Altium Designer, Cadence Allegro	None[1]	Limited access to some PLM objects (change, documents, etc) via REST
Siemens	Teamcenter X	NX, SolidEdge, SOLIDWORKS	Altium, Mentor	SAP[2] plus 3rd Party Integrations	Unlimited access
PTC	Windchill	CATIA V5, Creo, NX, SOLIDWORKS, Inventor and 3rd Party Integrations	3rd Party Integrations	3rd Party Integrations[3]	Unlimited access
Autodesk	Fusion Lifecycle	Integrations on-premises via Vault	EAGLE plus Integrations on-premises via Vault	JitterBit and 3rd Party Integrations	Unlimited access
Arena	Arena	SOLIDWORKS	Altium, Mentor, OrCAD	SAP Business ByDesign Integration as well as 3rd Party adapters and Public APIs	Unlimited access
Aras	Aras Innovator	SOLIDWORKS, CATIA V5, Creo, Inventor, AutoCAD, NX, SolidEdge	Altium, Cadence, Zuken, Mentor, Aucotec, EPLAN, Pulsonix, AutoCAD Electrical	Oracle ERP and Netsuite, SAP, QAD, MS Dynamics	Unlimited access
OpenBOM	OpenBOM	Onshape, SOLIDWORKS, Fusion360, Inventor, SolidEdge, NX, CATIA V5, Creo, KeyCreator	Altium Designer, EAGLE, Cadence Allegro and OrCAD	NetSuite included, Others as service offers	Unlimited access
Oracle	PLM Cloud	3rd Party Integrations	3rd Party Integrations	Via MuleSoft	Unlimited access
Propel	Propel PLM	SOLIDWORKS, via EPDM, Onshape	Coming soon	SAP via Force.com	Salesforce APIs Unlimited access
Upchain	Upchain	SOLIDWORKS, via EPDM, Onshape	EPLAN, AutoCAD Electrical, Promis.e	Via MuleSoft	Unlimited access

1 – JMS for iPaaS integration bus coming soon. 2 – Expect closer integration following co-selling agreement between SAP and Siemens in July 2020 3 – SAP has their own Windchill integration

Part 3 – Benefits of Cloud, Cloud Vendors and the Future

How can Cloud truly benefit PLM?

If it sounds like I am down on cloud-based PLM, it is just because I have seen many, many cases where pushing the cloud has been counter-productive. Are there cases where the cloud does fit and is beneficial?

- Social Enterprise

In the current context of the post-COVID world, we will be encouraged to work remotely more and more. This is really the sweet spot for cloud computing. I would argue that the essential processes of both internal and external collaboration are greatly enhanced by the cloud. These social aspects of **3D**EXPERIENCE platform are particularly powerful: connecting with users that have similar interests and competencies for knowledge sharing via 3DSwym, aggregating data via 3DDashboard and NetVibes, and sharing data with 3DDrive are all things that the cloud does astonishingly well. With solutions like **3D**EXPERIENCE platform, it is an all-or-nothing proposition: if you already use Slack or Chatter or Teams, there is no easy way to integrate them with **3D**EXPERIENCE on the cloud or to replace the Dassault app with one of these. Customers tend to be very hesitant to move from one collaboration platform to another and this lack of flexibility of **3D**EXPERIENCE platform on the cloud can be a handicap in this case. Let's hope that Teamcenter X and PTC Atlas will be a bit more flexible in how social enterprise software is integrated once more details are available about them. It would appear that with Active Workspace's flexible HTML5 frameworks, it would be rather easy to integrate other social collaboration tools, but I am unaware of any work in this area. Figure 19 below shows some of the places in the 3DDashboard where social enterprise functionality is used.

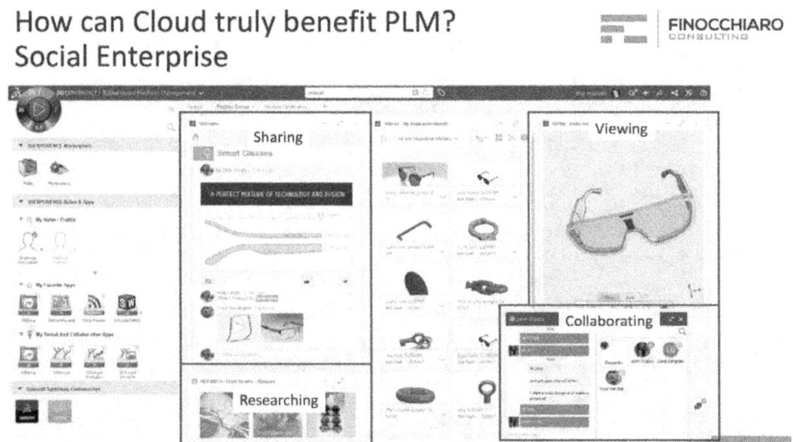

Figure 19 - 3DEXPERIENCE Platform Social Enterprise Features

Clearly, Microsoft Teams is changing the landscape of Enterprise Collaboration and the faster that PLM platforms adopt the new paradigm, the easier it will be for users to optimize their daily workflow. In Onshape, if a user clicks on a notification in Teams, it will open Onshape and go directly to the tagged feature on the 3D model. We should expect to see more of this leveraging of the tagging, notification and comments features of Teams going forward.

- Hybrid Clouds

To counter the objections mentioned above, ideally one would keep the heavy files on-premises and move the more collaborative processes to the cloud. I find this approach to be logical, and I recent tools such as OpenBOM or ShareAspace provide an excellent approach to integrating various bills of material over the cloud. Neither Siemens nor Dassault currently allows a hybrid between a SaaS offering and an on-premises file vault. PTC, however, does allow the SaaS version of Windchill to connect to local file servers for workgroups. Best of breed solutions will most likely blend the stability and configurability of on-premises platforms with lighter and more collaborative tools on the cloud.

Oracle Agile allows for their on-premises software to manage CAD files while the Oracle Cloud holds all the collaboration tools. Autodesk Fusion Lifecycle has a similar approach with Autodesk Vault on-premises and Fusion Lifecycle in the cloud.

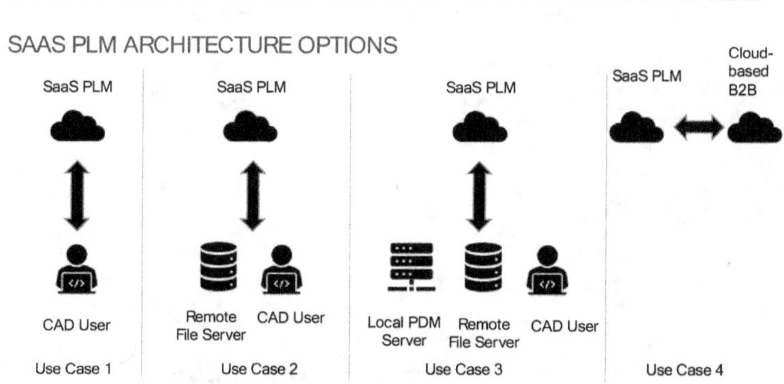

Figure 20 - Examples of SaaS PLM Architectures with Hybrids

As a summary, if we look at Figure 20, all the PLM vendors support Use Case 1 which is the most basic function of PLM after all, serving CAD users with PLM in the cloud. For Use Case 2, Siemens and PTC support having a local file server connected to an instance of their PLM in the cloud. For Use Case 3, Oracle Agile can connect to Oracle Product Hub on the cloud and Autodesk Vault can connect to Fusion Lifecycle on the cloud making these true hybrid systems. For Use Case 4, this is supposed to represent a multiple cloud scenario such as a SaaS PLM connecting to a SaaS ERP or CRM system. Propel PLM can obviously do this with Salesforce.com. Siemens announced an alliance with SAP to enable, among other things, better connections between Teamcenter X and SAP R/4HANA both on the cloud. PTC, Autodesk, and Aras have comprehensive REST API libraries that permit this kind of hybrid connection as well. Dassault Systèmes has announced an iPaaS gateway for this kind of exchange, but it has still not been released publicly.

- User Training

Another low-hanging fruit for cloud is the ease of training employees using the cloud. Gone are the windowless classrooms with under-desk PCs that you bump your knees against, sticky keyboards and legacy screens that allow nowhere on the tabletop to take notes and the whiteboard with years of previous learning still visible despite furious work with window cleaner and a dirty sponge. Now, using cloud, training can be done on the user's laptop in a classroom, at home, or in their office. I have taught many classes and appreciate that learning in a classroom where you can ask your teacher questions is more effective than self-paced learning. But with cloud and Teams, for example, you can teach the class remotely and have two-way communication with the teacher, so the experience of classroom teaching becomes replicable. Not to mention that in the post-COVID world, allowing folks to bone up on skills without getting exposed to the virus is a major benefit. SharePLM is one company that excels in remote training for PLM having designed the online training systems via the cloud for PLM companies and partners as well as PLM customers.

Companies like SharePLM, see Figure 21 below, take advantage of cloud platforms to make training and on-boarding of users much easier than traditional PowerPoint-driven classroom training. This allows for students anywhere and anytime to undergo training without risk of COVID contamination. It should be noted that the success of a PLM deployment depends heavily on an educated user community because if training if left too late in the process, people will not understand how or why they should change the way they work.

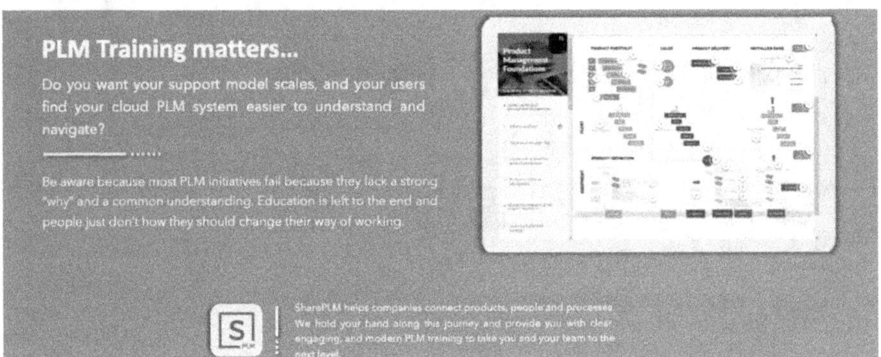

Figure 21 - SharePLM and Cloud Training

- Non-Production Environments

The cloud is ideal for situations where you need to stand up an environment in a very short period of time for Development, Proof of Concepts (POCs) or Technical Sandboxes. You can create an environment on the fly and have users tinker with it and take it for a test drive at lower cost than installing a full on-premises environment. Similarly, in the case of on-premises cloud where you have a rack of server blades with a sea of virtual machines, it is easy to clone environments and, say, test a new patch for quality and performance. With SaaS PLM on cloud, this is a could be an option depending on the flexibility of your cloud partner. AWS can easily do cloning in a PaaS scenario, but just to take an example, DS Public Cloud does not allow users to do so for their SaaS solutions. It is unknown at the time of this writing whether Teamcenter X or PTC Atlas will allow for cloning or not, but Teamcenter X does allow for moving all content from SaaS ("Base" or "Add-ons" to PaaS ("Personalized") and even down to IaaS or on-premises. For PaaS platforms such as Aras Innovator or PTC Windchill as a managed service, this is easily implemented. As noted earlier, some vendors like Autodesk offer

Enterprise tier licensing with prerelease sandboxes for integration testing. Figure 22 below shows a scenario of using Azure for disaster recovery.

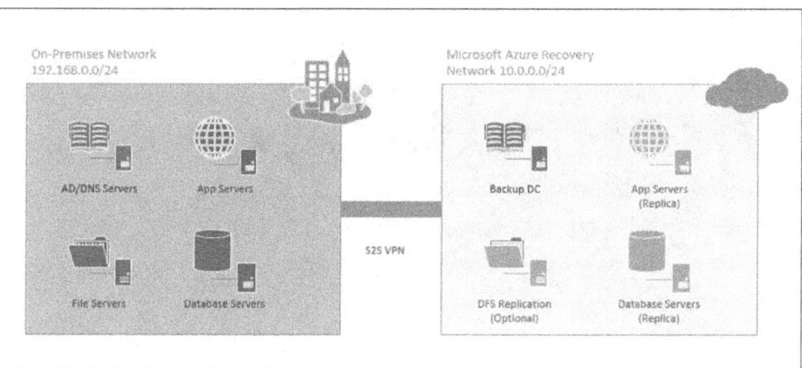

Figure 22 - Azure Example of Non-Production Environments for Disaster Recovery (https://www.itpromentor.com/azure-vnet/)

- Supply Chain Collaboration

One area where the cloud could be of enormous value in PLM is supply chain management. By removing the necessity for Tier N suppliers to access the OEM's network directly in order to facilitate the exchange of data and documentation, the cloud would make it far easier for B2B interactions. This presumes that the platform itself has a robust security and access system and additive and subtractive permissions on objects. What I mean by that is that if your full assembly is stored in a folder, you want to be able to allow access to sub-assemblies to a network of subcontractors without exposing the entire assembly. In some cases, you may want to build complex access control lists (ACLs) in order to determine which objects are visible to whom and at what period of their lifecycle. In **3DEXPERIENCE**, this is problematic because the Collaborative Spaces (DS name for folders, essentially) do not have granular security. In other words, everything in the space is either invisible or read-only or modifiable.You cannot protect individual objects or documents and you cannot have hierarchical spaces, making it quite complex to share sub-assemblies. Many customers have had to resort to workarounds using bookmarks, but as there is no customization possible, there is no way to program around the limitations.

Teamcenter and Windchill both allow for more granular access control via ACLs. But, perhaps the most innovative approach to this supply chain collaboration platform is Nova release of ShareAspace by Eurostep. OEMs and Suppliers can create collections which can in turn host multiple siloed spaces in which data to be shared can be held securely. What is unique is that the backend is a homegrown graph database rather than a relational database and that the granularity of access control can go all the way down to attribute level. This gives protection both to the OEM and to the Suppliers in all the exchanges.

In Figure 23 below, Eurostep explains how one of their customers leveraged their SaaS solution for a customer and their supply chain.

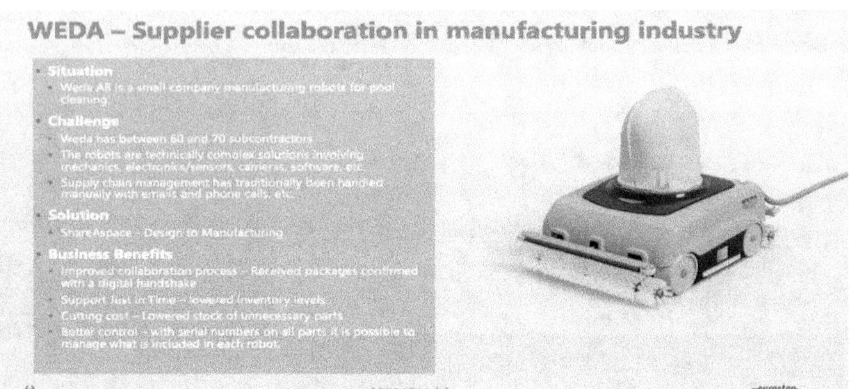

Figure 23 - WEDA Case Study for Eurostep and Supply Chain on SaaS Cloud

- Elastic and Burst Computing

One of the most exciting aspects of cloud computing is that it potentially removes any obstacles to practically infinite computing power and storage. With physical hardware, we are faced with the hard limit of the physical cores and gigabytes of memory installed in the dark, blinking racks in the subterranean machine room and typically the procurement process to add new hardware is long and arduous. Using the distributed, virtualized cloud technologies, it is of utmost simplicity to spin up additional cores and terabytes on the fly to make massive calculations or store temporary data during a calculation or data migration. This is one of the clearest differentiators for PLM and cloud, particularly in the area of simulation which can require hundreds of CPU cores and petabytes of storage to calculate and analyze the results of, say, an air tunnel or crash test to name just two examples. Also, as the manufacturing company grows organically through new product lines and inorganically through acquisitions, rather than re-source hardware for the data center for the expanding needs of the PLM system, cloud offers a seamless, elastic model for growing the PLM system along with the business. Figure 24 below shows how Siemens uses burst computing for their STAR-CCM computational fluid dynamics solution.

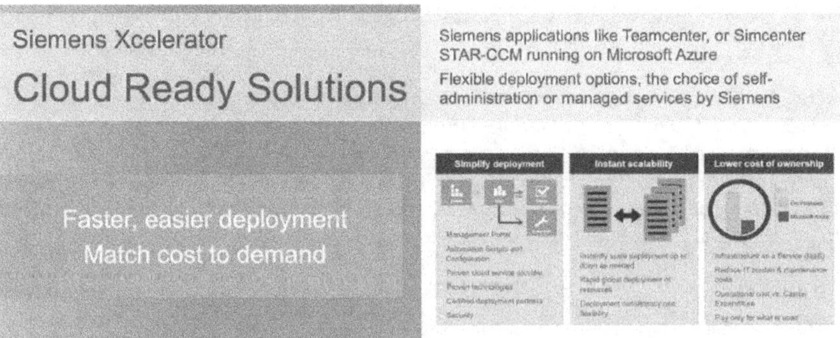

Figure 24 - Simcenter STAR-CCM using Azure for Burst Computing

- Flexible Pricing Models

Another advantage of cloud for PLM is that, as opposed to many on-premises pricing models, the licensing tends to be far more flexible. Solutions such as Upchain, Propel PLM, and Aras Innovator offer extremely simplified models of all-in pricing. Only dedicated adapters are priced separately, and all the core functionality of the full product portfolio is available for any paid user. For OpenBOM, the price is all-in, all CAD adapters are included. Typically, there is a free browsing/read-only license for adding outside or temporary participants and then a tiered model for adding users over time with the Enterprise tier offering benefits such as additional sandboxes and more release control. This way companies can truly have a simplified pricing rather than a complex matrix of roles and prices for their users allowing for more organic growth with fewer complications and lower cost.

Hardware providers such as Hewlett-Packard Enterprise (HPE), see Figure 25 below, have begun to change their economic models as well to convert them into SaaS mode. The Greenlake system from HPE allows customers to purchase hardware in their data center on a Pay-Per-Use model which also allows for transparent elasticity into the cloud for moving applications and data back and forth as the customer's business needs evolve. These architectures have been heavily exploited by SAP, but the potential is there for gains in PLM as well.

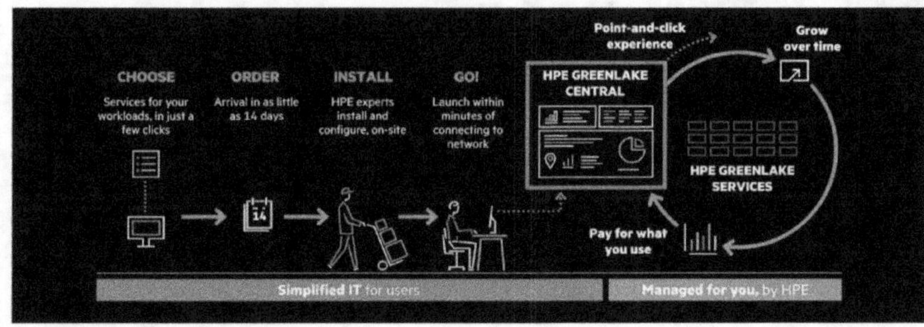

Figure 25 - HPE Greenlake Economic Model

- Full, Uninterrupted Digital Thread

Using many of the techniques already mentioned, especially burst computing and hybrid clouds, it is possible to ensure the continuity of your digital thread thanks to cloud computing. With the capacity to bridge multiple systems using REST, this ensures that the data flows seamlessly through the lifecycle of the product. In Figure 26 below, PTC shows their vision of digital thread where the digital twins on the bottom of the slide and the physical items on the top are connected end to end enabling advanced processes like Additive Manufacturing and Real-time IIoT simulation.

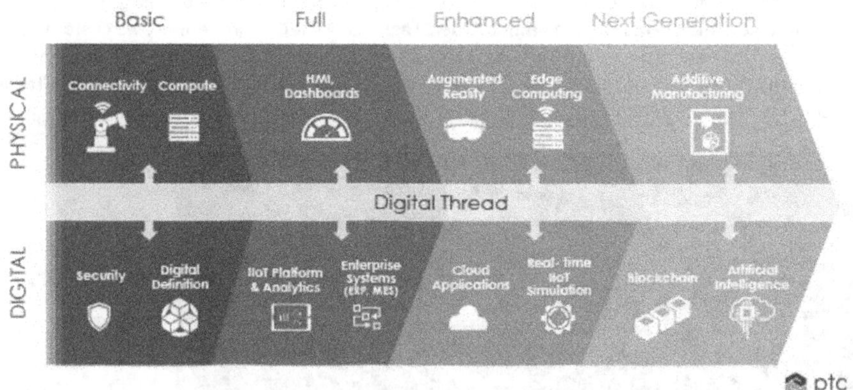

Figure 26 - PTC's View of Digital Thread

What are today's leading Cloud-based SaaS PLM platforms?

These will be grouped into three categories: Dassault, Siemens, PTC, and Aras are grouped together because they all are aimed at the world's largest manufacturing companies with the most comprehensive portfolios. Due to its massive revenue, I include Autodesk in this category and all of these vendors are listed in Table 13. Then comes Arena, OpenBOM, Oracle Product Lifecycle Cloud, SAP PLM, Propel PLM and Upchain as other niche and innovative cloud PLM vendors; then some special solutions such as Microsoft Excel, Eurostep's ShareAspace, Schwindt's verS-Cloud, and Ganister which I list in Table 14. Note that in the Table 13 below, I created columns to show the CAD solutions offered by the four biggest vendors and whether they require a downloadable rich client or whether the solution is entirely browser-based.

<u>Large and Diverse PLM Vendors</u>

Table 13 - Comparison of Offerings from Largest PLM Firms

CLOUD PLM VENDORS WITH WIDEST INDUSTRY COVERAGE

Vendor	Location	Estimated Yearly Revenue	Privately Held or Publicly Traded	SaaS Offering	Primary Cloud Provider(s) ranked by preference	Primary CAD	CAD is Rich Client or Browser-based?	Search-based Front End
Dassault Systèmes	France	~$4B	Publicly Traded but Majority of Shares held by Insiders	3DEXPERIENCE	Outscale, AWS, Huawei[1]	CATIA 3DEXP	Rich Client	3DDashboard
						X Design	Browser-based	
						SOLIDWORKS	Rich Client	
PTC	USA (Boston)	$1.16B	Publicly Traded on NASDAQ	Windchill	Azure, AWS	Creo	Rich Client	ThingWorx Navigate[2]
				Onshape[3]	AWS	Onshape	Browser-based	Onshape
Siemens Digital Industries Software	Germany	~$4B	Publicly Traded	Teamcenter X	AWS, Azure	NX	Rich Client	Active Workspace
						SolidEdge	Rich Client	
Autodesk	USA (San Francisco)	~$3.4B	Publicly Traded	Fusion Lifecycle	Azure	Fusion 360	Browser-based	N/A
						Inventor	Rich Client	
Aras	USA (Boston)	~$100M	Privately Held	N/A	Azure	CAD Agnostic	N/A	N/A

Notes:
1 - Huawei cloud only available inside China for **3D**EXPERIENCE. Note that here is an Outscale datacenter in Hong Kong.
2 - ThingWorx Navigate from PTC's IOT brand ThingWorx can be used as a lighter navigator aid to Windchill
3 - Atlas platform still under development (announced early June 2020)

- Dassault Systèmes 3DEXPERIENCE platform on DS Public Cloud

The **3D**EXPERIENCE platform is the most mature SaaS PLM on the market with the broadest portfolio. Built on the core of ENOVIA V6 kernel, it is a business platform with product lifecycle management apps coming from the CATIA, ENOVIA, SIMULIA, DELMIA, and BIOVIA brands. It covers product design from conception to manufacturing. In addition to 3DSpace (the server environment supporting these features), it adds social enterprise features using 3DSwym, user dashboarding via 3DDashboard, and it includes analytics, messaging, identity management, and visualization. No other vendor comes close, yet, to the diverse portfolio offered on DS public cloud.

However, despite adding loads of new functionality via the acquisitions of EXALEAD, NetVibes, and other core technology to create the **3D**EXPERIENCE platform, the core of the platform was never re-architected and still has some features (mentioned above) that are antithetical to a multi-tenant environment (triggers, JPOs, property files, etc). Lastly, I mentioned above that the integration of **3D**EXPERIENCE on cloud with external systems such as ERP is not yet based on microservices and is, at the time of this writing, still not generally available (GA) making the management end-to-end of the digital thread problematic.

We spoke of burst computing above where punctually running large simulations could be economically more efficient by "bursting" them into the cloud where resources can be allocated and deallocated far easier than on premises. Until recently, this was problematic for **3D**EXPERIENCE. Traditionally, SIMULIA's computational software ABAQUS uses a token-based model where tokens with a set number of compute units (say, for example, measured in the number of nodes on a structure) were purchased on a yearly basis and consumed during on-premises calculations and returned to a reusable pool. This was unwieldly and too expensive to implement on cloud as the compute (CPU cores) and storage (disk space) resources had to be purchased separately by the customer. Also, the official DS cloud vendor Outscale did not have adequate hardware for high performance computing (HPC) and DS had been attempting to reuse their file collaboration server (FCS) from their PLM platform for data storage which created performance issues as well. As a result, there were few compelling reasons for customers to use the cloud for burst computing.

In the current R2021x release, they have transparently introduced a new compute backend utilizing appropriate Cloud instance types, simplified licensing in the form of Cloud Compute Credits or tokens, which now may be used for both the computational hardware with the software compute units, and, for 3DEXPERIENCE simulation. This new compute backend design has effectively removed the bidirectional file transfer requirements to and from and FCS for results storage. Calculations are classified into Small, Medium and Large depending on how complex the operations are. Customers then purchase packs of Cloud Compute Credits (CCD-OC) and cloud storage (PBG-OC) and consume them at their ease until they are out of credits. A Cloud token model is available as well so that customers may also continue to use tokens for their on-premises or on cloud calculations. Currently, only structural analysis of **3D**EXPERIENCE models can leverage this infrastructure, but plans are to first add Computational Fluid Dynamics and to later enable the non-**3D**EXPERIENCE packages such as ABAQUS, CST, and POWERFLOW as well.

Dassault is working to bring more brands into their **3D**EXPERIENCE portfolio including their life sciences brand BIOVIA and their earth sciences brand GEOVIA. In 2019, they announced **3D**EXPERIENCE WORKS which is a pared-down platform aimed at the SOLIDWORKS installed base. This includes pieces of ENOVIA for change management, SIMULIA for simulation management, DELMIA for manufacturing planning and leveraging their acquisition of IQMS in order to offer a small but complete ERP solution aimed at small to medium enterprises.

- Siemens Digital Industry Software Teamcenter X

Siemens claimed in their announcements in June 2020 that Teamcenter X is truly microservices-based which gives them a great advantage in terms of integration and thus digital continuity. (Note that the "X" stands for "Xcelerator portfolio" and not the number "10".) The Mendix low-code platform makes it easy to create apps on the fly which leverage features from the Teamcenter core. The "Base" offering includes fundamental PLM capabilities such as Revision Control, Workflow, Document Management, BOM Management and Visualization. Current option add-on SaaS packaged solutions include mechanical and electrical CAD integrations (SOLIDWORKS, NX, Mentor, Altium, etc (see Figure 28)) plus Change Management and Classification. This list of add-ons will continue to grow from release to release.

At any time, customers can, via request for quote, opt to add-in more SaaS packaged solutions pulled from the Teamcenter portfolio which they call "Personalized" offering. In this case, Teamcenter X leverages Teamcenter business logic running as a managed instance (single tenant) and uses underlying multi-tenant services from the Mendix Cloud platform for file management and authentication. Personalized solutions would be applied to the Teamcenter business logic running as a managed instance, but would continue leveraging the underlying multi-tenant services from the Mendix Cloud Platform, similar to how other SaaS packaged add-ins are managed by Teamcenter X.

Mendix, as mentioned above, is a scripting engine which is independent from but compatible with Teamcenter X. It allows for access into the Teamcenter X APIs but also those of their IOT portfolio, Mindsphere. It also features an App Store which is public, but customers can also create their own private App Stores, which is unique in the SaaS PLM market today as far as my research has shown. Another powerful advantage is how Mendix can also bring MindSphere IOT data to bear and the flexible Active Workspace leveraging a search-led UI for efficient, stream-lined user interfaces. They also added an AI-powered Assistant for optimizing user navigation (also available on-premises) based on their use of Teamcenter as well as their team's use of the portfolio – a trend also touted by Upchain and Propel PLM. It will be interesting to see how the SaaS flavor Teamcenter X portfolio grows in the future.

The Simulation Process and Data Management (SPDM) solution on top of Teamcenter called "Teamcenter Simulation" is also on the PaaS-style managed cloud environment. This enables customers to deploy their SPDM solution on the cloud. Several analysis products in the Simcenter portfolio – Simcenter 3D, Simcenter Nastran, Simcenter Amesim, and Simcenter STAR-CCM+ can be accessed via their strategic partnership with Rescale[32] to use burst computing on the cloud.

Teamcenter has a multi-site offer which allows federation of multiple Teamcenter instances up to the project level, the BOM level or the assembly level in which a single Teamcenter instance can manage the metadata of the parts stored in the local vault of the other instances. Teamcenter X also features several preconfigured workflow templates. The core non-functional characteristics are speed, security, always up to date, highly available, highly compatible and fixed price. With Teamcenter X, Siemens has staked a critical place in the SaaS PLM market.

---

[32] https://www.plm.automation.siemens.com/global/en/our-story/newsroom/simcenter-saas-cloud-offering/66009

- PTC Windchill, Onshape and Atlas

Even before the introduction of Windchill 11 in 2016, the entire PTC Windchill portfolio has been available in mono-tenant SaaS mode as well as a managed service (or PaaS) or on-premises. By default, the SaaS or managed service is deployed on Microsoft Azure, but customers can also choose to deploy on AWS. PTC's investments in supporting Windchill on Azure and AWS are also made available to customers that still prefer to traditionally manage the software themselves. It is possible to move from the SaaS platform to the PaaS platform rather easily. Hybrid solutions with local data storage is also a possibility. The SaaS pricing model which includes licenses for both software and operations was put in place in 2018.

The Managed Service/PaaS offering allows for flexibility if customers want to pay for the software using a subscription model and for the hardware using a more traditional capital expenditure model. It is all up to how best it fits the customer's financial requirements and there are not technical limitations. It must be emphasized that in each of these cases, it is the full portfolio that is available and not merely a subset. Managed Services customers have a cloud portal for managing aspects of their environment such as checking on availability and restarting services as well as managing their development and preproduction testing environments for those that are managing a more customized deployment.

PTC's Vuforia platform for augmented reality is a multi-tenant solution as well and fully integrated into their Windchill and ThingWorx platforms. Also, PTC does bundle a preconfigured version of Windchill supporting mandatory processes and regulatory submissions (FDA, EU, etc.) for Medical Device manufacturers that is full-on SaaS and regularly audited for compliance.

In 2013, PTC acquired the company NetIDEAS which had already been their preferred PaaS platform for deploying Windchill in the cloud. The 2019 acquisition of Onshape gave PTC a fully cloud-based CAD system with some limited data management. In June 2020, PTC announced its forthcoming Atlas platform which will be their cloud backend blending the best practices from NetIDEAS and the infrastructure behind Onshape. It will eventually be the common backend for its entire cloud portfolio providing deployment, security, identification and authentication and other common services to be consumed by apps running on Atlas. Initially, it is targeted for Onshape and Vuforia customers, but in short order, Windchill and other PTC brands will be added as additional SaaS apps available on the Atlas platform. Each of the apps will have logic for encrypting all data at rest using the customer's own keys. The goals of Atlas include a continuous development environment where new features are delivered weekly and patches can be delivered just hours after problem resolution.

As a corporate platform for PTC, Atlas will provide:
- An internal operational excellence view so that their community of over 2000 developers has a consistent common developer operations (DevOps) platform with containers and optimizations which drastically reduces development and deployment time for new functionality and security patches and enables their Continuous Improvement/Continuous Deployment (CI/CD) initiatives
- A customer experience view where the continuity of the entire digital thread can be ensured end-to-end allowing customers to leverage the full power of the PTC portfolio

Bonus: Creo customers will be reassured to know that they will gradually get new features coming from Onshape, but that Creo will remain the CAD system of choice for medium to large scale enterprises, while Onshape will focus on new customers in the broader 3D CAD market, particularly those with new and innovative development processes and programs. Onshape will also be also integrated to Windchill for

Engineering Bill of Materials (EBOM), Manufacturing Bills of Materials (MBOM) and Enterprise Change Management (ECM) so that hybrid assemblies will be possible. Onshape also features an infinite undo list with an unlimited number of participants with version control and branch management, analogous to how software is managed within Software Configuration Management (SCM) tools like Git. Said differently, customers will likely choose to continue using Creo for the overall workflow and will leverage Onshape for Agile product development or newer projects.

- Autodesk Fusion Lifecycle and Fusion 360

As opposed to DS, PTC and Siemens mentioned above, Autodesk has focused primarily on Building Information Management (BIM) in the construction industry and on a narrow range of manufacturing industries (Industrial Machinery & Products, Consumer Electronics & High Tech, and Automotive Suppliers & Components). Also, in their portfolio, the focus on a core list of functionalities (New Product Introduction, BOM, Change and Quality Management, Supplier Collaboration and Product Data Management) with their multi-tenant Fusion Lifecyle PLM suite. It integrates to a wide range of external applications (Netsuite, Oracle, SalesForce, SAP, Microsoft Dynamics, and SOLIDWORKS PDM), but primarily addresses customers that have already chosen Autodesk as their CAD platform, and without pretentions to encroach on simulation without external integrations. Fusion Lifecycle can be connected to on-premises Autodesk Vault PDM systems as well.

Fusion Lifecycle does not include social enterprise functionality and limited analytics on PLM data but have REST interfaces for extracting data for external analysis. Some adapters exist from JitterBit. Autodesk Fusion Lifecycle has one unique per user/per year price for all platform functionality and features with only external adapters (CAD, ERP, etc) being paid add-ons.

Fusion 360 is their cloud-based CAD tool which competes with Onshape and SOLIDWORKS X Design allowing for 3D modeling with a web browser and no specific graphics hardware. It is aimed at electronics and high tech and has a strong manufacturing flavor with capabilities for additive manufacturing (3D printing), NC machining, and robotics.

- Aras Innovator

Of the products in this book, Aras is the only one which is cloud-ready but does not yet have a SaaS or multi-tenant offer. By their own estimates, about 24% of their customers are using Aras on the cloud. Their strategy has been to leverage the Azure Marketplace to easily deploy Aras Innovator Virtual Machines into the cloud in just minutes. Their platform is a bit broader than those of Autodesk or Propel because they include some simulation and better CAD integration. But what really sets Aras apart is their flexible data modeling and thus the rapidity of deployment without impacting upgrades or customizations. While most upgrades are measured in weeks, the length of the upgrade cycle is usually dictated by a company's ability to test and implement the upgrade. One of their most comprehensive and customized deployments at a large software company was completed in just three days. They achieve this via their modular architecture with isolated layers for Unified Data Modeling, the Modeling Engine and Platform Services.

Their cloud offering, which is currently a PaaS but being evolved towards a SaaS, is particularly focused on the top 900 manufacturing companies where they have had several recent successes: they are going directly after Dassault, PTC and Siemens customers which is another unique aspect of Aras.

Another original thing about Aras is that it is open and free to download. When a customer decides to subscribe, they will be entitled to Aras executed upgrades, unlimited training and other benefits. All Innovator applications are included in the subscription so there are no additional software costs as a company adds new Aras functionality over time. Professional services and/or external integrations to ERP or CAD systems are available at additional cost. This approach has led Aras to a 40% annual growth primarily due to word of mouth where users of one of billion dollar vendors (DS, PTC, Siemens) will download it for free and play around and eventually negotiate with Aras to displace their existing system as has happened at Microsoft, Airbus, GE and other large firms.

<u>**Niche and Innovative Cloud SaaS PLM Vendors**</u>

Table 14 - Niche and Innovative Cloud SaaS PLM Vendors

NICHE AND INNOVATIVE CLOUD SAAS PLM VENDORS

Vendor	Location	Estimated Yearly Revenue	Privately Held or Publicly Traded	Primary Cloud Provider	Primary Industries Covered
Arena	USA (San Francisco)	~$36M	Privately Held	AWS	High Tech, Med Devices, Cons. Elec
OpenBOM	USA (Boston)	<$1M	Privately Held	AWS	Modestly-sized Manufacturing Projects
Oracle PLM Cloud	USA (San Francisco)	~$40B	Privately Held	Oracle	Mostly document-centric industries[1]
Propel PLM	USA (San Francisco)	~$7.5M	Privately Held	Salesforce	High Tech, Med Devices, Cons. Packaged Goods
Upchain	Canada (Toronto)	~$2M	Privately Held	AWS	Any "tribal" company
Microsoft Excel & Teams	USA (Seattle)	~$125B	Privately Held	Azure / Office365	All companies
Eurostep ShareASpace	Sweden	~$10M	Privately Held	Azure	High value supply chain collaboration
Schwindt verS-Cloud	Germany	N/A	Privately Held	Azure	Small to tiny manufacturing companies
Ganister	France	N/A	Privately Held	AWS	Small to tiny manufacturing companies

NOTES:
1 - Banking and Insurance, Communications, Engineering and Construction, Food and Beverage, Healthcare, Hospitality, Life Sciences, Public Sector, Retail, Utilities

- Arena Solutions

Arena is another multi-tenant SaaS PLM platform which is, like Propel, focused on High Tech and Medical Devices. They seem to have one of the most diverse integrations across multiple disciplines including a wide variety of ERP solutions, EDA and MCAD, Electronic Component Databases, CRM, and Quality Assurance & Control. One interesting differentiator is that they are the only vendor I found to talk about training records and compliance on their website. They also tout an analytics system. They do not have a manufacturing or simulation footprint and the principal CAD system they connect to is SOLIDWORKS. And, like Propel, they claim to have deep knowledge of regulatory compliance, a critical piece in the industries they serve. But, like Propel, they remain a niche player for smaller, less complex assemblies.

- OpenBOM

Oleg Shilovitsky's OpenBOM has made some waves in the cloud-based SaaS PLM space. OpenBOM is a partner with multiple CAD, PLM, and ERP vendors including Autodesk, Dassault SOLIDWORKS, Onshape, PTC, Siemens Solid Edge, Oracle NetSuite, and others. OpenBOM is a multi-tenant, SaaS PLM hosted on AWS cloud which initially was centered on collaborating on Bills of Materials, but has since expanded to include change management, CAD integrations[33] for SOLIDWORKS, Autodesk Fusion 360, Autodesk Inventor, Solid Edge, Onshape, Eagle, and Altium Designer, as well as vendor management. OpenBOM unique data sharing capabilities allow sharing of the data with anyone who has an OpenBOM account while also ensuring IP protection via access rights. One key advantage of OpenBOM is its pricing model ranging from $25/month to $375/month with no limit on the number of users and the proactive support that they provide to their customers. It is not yet a full digital thread/digital twin implementation but is an excellent choice for smaller scoped projects over a flexible time period. The fact that at any time you can extract all your data to move it elsewhere is a nice reassurance against vendor lock-in and also means that it is easy to push data to downstream manufacturing systems.

---

[33] http://openbom.com/integrations

- Oracle Agile and Oracle Product Development Cloud

Oracle has had a tortuous PLM roadmap after a series of acquisitions and some confusion as to positioning. Currently, they have Oracle Agile on-premises for classic PDM-style data management (despite not having a native CAD tool), document management, and configuration management. They are particularly present in formula-based industries such as pharmaceuticals and consumer processed goods as well as high-tech, all industries with more document-based requirements. Oracle's Product Development Cloud is a multi-tenant SaaS platform which has the more collaborative PLM processes and can connect to Oracle Agile on-premises. It is focused on Innovation and aimed at Portfolio Management, Supply Chain Management and Requirements Management processes in the same industries mentioned for Agile.

- SAP PLM

I normally should have done a deeper dive on SAP-PLM in this paper as well, but on July 15, 2020, SAP and Siemens announced a co-selling agreement where SAP sells Teamcenter for PLM and Siemens sells Intelligent Asset Management solution ("plant management system"), as well as SAP's Project and Portfolio Management. This spells the end to the somewhat confusing life of SAP-PLM. It will be interesting to see what other blends come down the pipe because SAP S/4HANA is an incredibly powerful cloud automation system with built-in AI and machine learning, most likely superior to that behind Teamcenter X. Also, Active Workspace of Teamcenter truly resembles the SAP Fiori user experience, so will SAP adopt Active Workspace or vice-versa? One also wonders of the fate of the excellent visualization tool Right Hemisphere which SAP acquired in 2011. I suspect that it will remain a tool for visualizing their analytics but that Siemens tools will be used on 3D CAD. In any case, this sounds like outstanding news for both customers of Teamcenter and SAP.

- Propel PLM

Propel PLM leverages the powerful DNA of SalesForce's multi-tenant cloud architecture and platform to create an innovative cloud-only platform. Like Fusion Lifecycle, it is focused on High Tech as well as the Medical Devices and Consumer Packaged Goods markets. As such, the platform is more shifted towards bringing products to market with up-to-date information than the conception and engineering phases. They are also clearly pushing into heavily regulated markets and thus have a flexible and comprehensive compliancy story.

The Propel founders designed Propel PLM with three use cases in mind:

- Use Case 1: Engineer to Order (ETO) application which combines capabilities in Propel with Salesforce Manufacturing Cloud: take an order, acquire quotes, commit to delivery, configure the product, modify product tied to a project including R&D cost, manufacturing cost, push into price book with availability dates.
- Use Case 2: After-sales Service leveraging the Salesforce Field Service Lightning/Management Cloud (an MRO solution) giving control over the product record with change management. For example, a user can push changes for upgrade with statements like "latest of everything but these two, and fix power supply appropriately."
- User Case 3: Defect Management and Customer Care Management

- Upchain

Another relative newcomer in the SaaS PLM market is Upchain, first released in 2017 with the explicit intention to be disruptive. Founder John Laslavic saw how in the automotive market, the original equipment manufacturers (OEMs) were vertically integrated which made too many assumptions of proximity between the principal factories and the suppliers. This model is no longer relevant in the 21st century and therefore Upchain was designed for a far more horizontal, fragmented and heterogeneous ecosystem.

Upchain features a unique 16-sided data model which allows for combining things easily and creating virtual profiles on the fly. The intention was to recreate the ease of adaptation and modeling that MatrixOne had before their acquisition by Dassault. It consists of a modern architecture with the intention not to fall into the trap of tailoring a solution for one specific client and essentially painting themselves into a corner. The solution is multi-tenant hosted on AWS with all features available to all users with an on-off style of activation and integrations based on Mulesoft. It has a free view-only tier and three cost tiers: $30 - $70 - $200 per user per month.

Upchain has a unique program called Connect the Chain wherein they on-board their customers into a virtual environment where they are led through different PLM phases for creating BOM variants, change management, supplier management, design reviews, data discovery and analysis – all part of a teaching institution for certifying Upchain users directly on the Upchain platform. Graduates with an agreement become real commercial subscribers of Upchain. During the COVID pandemic, the company offered additional licenses to Connect the Chain alumni.

Another unique idea behind Upchain is that manufacturing companies, particularly smaller more agile ones, work in a "tribal" model with groups which are discrete and semi-autonomous. They are aimed at companies for which externally procured sub-assemblies account for between 40% and 70% of their designs because under 40% tends to be very CAD heavy and over 70% becomes more of a procurement solution rather than a PLM solution. As such, they integrated natively into Microsoft Office apps like Excel and Word and are able to maintain the data record and revise numbers automatically while providing viewing and annotation of CAD models and a robust ideation platform.

Smaller, but interesting alternatives

- Microsoft Excel + Microsoft Teams

OK, so I am being a little provocative here, but if we are honest, probably 90% of PLM today is done by Excel and as more companies migrated to Office365 and as Microsoft phases out SharePoint and Skype for Business, clearly PLM vendors will have to deal with Excel and Teams for years to come.

- Eurostep ShareAspace Server

Eurostep is a Swedish systems integrator and software developer who has focused on exchange standards, mainly STEP and PLCS, for over thirty years. Their ShareAspace product on the cloud allows for supplier collaboration in an innovative manner with finely grained access controls. They created the product to be cloud-native with an understanding that collaboration needs to be multi-user, multi-organization, multi-company in order to be efficient. Unlike the other small and medium sized players mentioned here, Eurostep's customers tend to be large Aerospace companies, Defense companies, Automobile companies and increasingly Architecture, Engineering and Construction firms. Their backend features a graph database which allows for in-memory access to documents and metadata preserving relationships between the objects. Technologies used are the most modern and besides the graph database include the use of REST APIs, soft types, microservices and detailed security. Both suppliers and OEMs can protect all their data all the way down to individual attributes. In general, the pricing is based on the number of partners to be connected. It is a fascinating approach to digital thread and twin which maintains the PDM, ERP and MRO systems in place and only pulls the data for collaboration into the cloud and pushes changes back out.

Teamcenter and Windchill both allow for granular access control via ACLs. But, perhaps the most innovative approach to this supply chain collaboration platform is ShareAspace by Eurostep. OEMs and suppliers can create collections which can in turn host multiple siloed spaces in which data to be shared can be held securely. What is unique is that the backend is a graph database rather than a relational database and thus the granularity of access control can go all the way down to attribute level. This gives IP protection both to the OEM and to the Suppliers in all the exchanges.

- Schwindt's vierS-Cloud

Schwindt is a small Dassault reseller in Germany that struck on an excellent idea: why not build a PLM toolbox using an open source graph database and integrated with common tools such as Microsoft Teams. Their customer base tends to have a handful of CATIA seats and cannot afford the luxury of an expensive marquee platform like **3D**EXPERIENCE, Windchill or Teamcenter. Also, the market has seen a massive movement of companies of all sizes towards Office365 as well as Teams and, for the most part, this has not really been fully taken into account by the major PLM vendors. vierS-Cloud (as in "vier" (the German word for "four") S's: "Simple Smart Schwindt Solution") is built on standard microservices with standard Microsoft components such as Active Directory for identity management and PostgreSQL for the database and covers most of the classic PLM functions such as BOM and Change Management. It is more of a service offering for connecting the dots in a small organization than a full-fledged PLM, but it got me to thinking about how we can use PLM "in conjunction with" as opposed to "instead of" our favorite word processor, presentation editor, spreadsheet program, and enterprise collaboration tool.

- Ganister

Yoann Maingon left Aras in 2018 and after cutting his teeth at a few Aras-related startups decided in August 2020 to create a new PLM platform that he baptized Ganister. He noted that many divisions in aircraft and car manufacturers were relatively far away from the CAD departments and had a need for PLM that was not being addressed by the big CAD-centric vendors. He also remarked that many of the PLM systems are trying to oblige customers to use a pre-baked PLM and adapt their business model to it rather than the other way around. He built Ganister with Node.js for the application server and leveraging Neo4j for the database all on AWS infrastructure with S3 storage for files. The data model is highly flexible as it is based on a graph database[34] which makes asking questions like "where is this part used and how deeply in the assembly" is made easy and fast via the Cypher query language. They would like to be seen as a toolkit for PLM system integrators and are focused on configuration management for now. Their plan is to build up an ecosystem of partners and build up custom solutions which remain easy to maintain and highly scalable using the latest cloud technologies. It is a bold move, but Yoann told me that he feels that the market needs to be more agile and that graph-based models are the right direction for PLM in the 21st century.

---

[34] A graph database is different from a traditional Relational Database (RDMS) in that rather than storing data in rows and columns and writing queries to build relationships between the objects, data items in the store are related to a collection of nodes, edges, and properties representing the relationships between the nodes. This allows for extremely fast querying of relationships since they are perpetually stored in the database.

The Future of PLM and Cloud

Further Consolidation, Cooperation, and Acquisitions

The next five-year window will certainly see a rapid maturing of the SaaS PLM space with some of the smaller players certainly being absorbed by the larger ones and with more comprehensive product portfolios from the latest entrants into the game. The new cooperation agreements of Siemens and SAP will result in some creative solutions blending Teamcenter X and SAP R/4HANA on the cloud. The market is still somewhat fragmented around newer markets like Retail. Dassault snapped up Centric in 2018 to help rebuild their Retail and Fashion industry vertically, but they have yet to propose Centric as a SaaS solution. This market has lots of embedded players like Lectra and Gerber which were traditionally more on-premises solutions but have started to introduce SaaS solutions, and, with new cloud-only solutions like Bombyx, further consolidation can be expected here as well.

Artificial Intelligence

Vendors like Siemens and Upchain are already integrating Artificial Intelligence (AI) into the navigation for their user interfaces and certainly other vendors will follow up on that idea. But the more critical application today is probably in the field of generative design where Dassault Systèmes and PTC have already been using AI for training and testing new models creating some truly mind-bending experiences. AI will also come increasingly into play in the manufacturing space for robotics as well as the technology matures. Vendors like PTC who can leverage the AI capabilities of Azure will reduce direct cost while consuming AI as a commodity rather than doing all the development in-house. This is definitely a field to watch. Cloud offers the scalability and elasticity that AI systems need to run efficiently, and it is a natural place to see the big advances take place. In supporting the value creation process, Stephan Clambaneva, Chief Innovation Officer at iD8ters is promoting the idea of using AI to reward designers and engineers based on the impact of their work on the overall efficiency and innovative nature of the products they work on.

Analytics

Several of the vendors, particularly Siemens and Dassault Systèmes have tried to augment their analytics capabilities on the cloud via their CAMSTAR Omneo[35] and EXALEAD acquisitions[36] respectively. Dassault has also heavily invested in graph database technology startup NuoDB[37] and will continue to integrate analytics into their 3DDashboard. It is expected that most vendors will need to add advanced analytics to their portfolios. Siemens in particular could have a big advantage if they leverage SAP's Qualtrics acquisition[38] in the context of the recent agreements between those two German software giants. Propel PLM can leverage the built-in analytics of Salesforce as well following the recent acquisition of Tableau by the latter[39]. Analytics have traditionally been used for rollups on change management and part reuse analysis, but cost calculations and what-if analysis will become more prevalent over time as well as preventive maintenance as it relates to IOT. Using the cloud for analytics will give relatively unlimited scalability for calculations as well as easier methods of sharing and presenting the results to various audiences using modern user interfaces.

---

[35] https://www.plm.automation.siemens.com/global/en/our-story/newsroom/siemens-press-release/43785

[36] https://www.3ds.com/press-releases/single/dassault-systemes-acquires-exalead/

[37] https://www.datanami.com/2014/02/26/dassault_picks_nuodb_to_back_new_cloud_offerings/

[38] https://www.enterprisetimes.co.uk/2018/11/12/sap-spends-8-billion-on-qualtrics/

[39] https://www.enterprisetimes.co.uk/2019/06/11/salesforce-doubles-down-against-sap-with-tableau-acquisition/

Expanded Footprints

PLM has been expanding beyond product design and engineering for over two decades already as simulation and manufacturing are brought into the portfolios for most of the vendors. PTC's acquisition of ThingWorx[40] and the creation of MindSphere by Siemens[41] has also brought the world of IOT into the PLM's sphere of influence. Some of the other enterprise processes such as Customer Relationship Management will certainly also get closer to PLM with more direct customer feedback to R&D as well as leveraging supplier information more efficiently. For the cloud, this means better utilization of computing, storage and network resources as the digital thread expands across the enterprise to envelop the cradle-to-grave product development processes.

New Markets

PLM has been well-anchored in the Aerospace and Defense, Transportation, Industrial Equipment, Medical Devices, and High-Tech industries for a few decades already. Despite the near stranglehold on the Architecture and Construction market that Autodesk maintains, Dassault has been trying to make inroads by adapting CATIA and **3D**EXPERIENCE to cover not just buildings but mining (via their GEOVIA brand[42]) and city planning (via their 3DEXPERIENCity brand[43]). I mentioned Fashion and Retail having lots of smaller players already as well as heavy presence from PTC's FlexPLM and Dassault's Centric[44]. PLM will also try to address newer markets in order to create new income streams because there are still industries that could benefit from PLM but have not yet had a compelling reason to look at it. The availability of SaaS PLM for less tech savvy markets will truly push cloud adoption as the PLM systems become more affordable and also easier to understand because of the more modern user interfaces and accessibility via the cloud.

Marketplaces

Teamcenter X has promised new public and private marketplaces based on their Mendix App Store[45]. Dassault Systèmes' **3D**EXPERIENCE already has marketplaces for part suppliers and engineering shops[46]. PTC has an app marketplace[47] as well. This is one place where the cloud really excels and platform approaches like PTC's forthcoming Atlas platform and Propel PLM's reliance on Force.com will be real advantages. The cloud is truly built for creating exchanges between companies and we can expect that more and more PLM vendors will open their platforms to allow for more commoditization of services.

---

[40] https://investor.ptc.com/index.php/news-releases/news-release-details/ptc-acquires-leading-internet-things-platform-provider-thingworx

[41] https://press.siemens.com/global/en/pressrelease/siemens-strengthens-its-iot-operating-system-mindsphere-through-technology-partnership

[42] https://www.3ds.com/products-services/geovia/products/?woc=%7B%22category%22%3A%5B%22category%2Fproduct-tips-and-tricks%22%5D%7D

[43] https://www.3ds.com/stories/how-can-technology-shape-the-future/imagining-more-sustainable-city/

[44] https://www.3ds.com/press-releases/single/dassault-systemes-and-centric-software-come-together-to-accelerate-digital-transformation-of-fashio/

[45] https://appstore.mendix.com

[46] https://www.3ds.com/3dexperience/marketplace/

[47] https://www.ptc.com/en/marketplace

Augmented Reality / Virtual Reality (AR/VR)

PTC has a lead in the AR/VR space with their Vuforia product line, but the other vendors – particularly those with native CAD systems – are sure to follow through on the promise of this technology. With the necessity of maintaining social distancing due to the COVID pandemic, technologies which allow hands-on collaboration without the physical contact such as the Vuforia Chalk AR[48] app will be more and more business critical over time. I have noted elsewhere that Vuforia is fully multi-tenant and SaaS already. It is likely that over time, AR/VR will have as massive an impact on designing new products as it has had on the gaming industry[49].

Additive Manufacturing and 3D Printing

Additive manufacturing will certainly also become far more important and its integration into the CAD systems will play a critical role in the "buy" vs "make" decisions made later. The **3D**EXPERIENCE platform already allows users to order 3d printed parts via their marketplace. Using the cloud to bring people and processes together and also trying to reduce the ecological footprint of manufacturing will drive even more innovation in this swiftly moving direction which has lots of players such as Carbon3D[50] are reducing the footprint of the 3d printers while augmenting their capacity to create stunning products. There is likely to be some consolidation here as well, where it would not be surprising to see some of the big PLMs acquiring smaller players.

Collaboration

All manners of remote collaboration, virtual white boards, virtual meetings, etc. are of prime importance so that future pandemics have as low an impact as possible on engineering and design and so predominant sharing and collaboration platforms like Microsoft Teams will have to be seamlessly integrated into the PLM platforms to avoid discontinuity and user confusion. Dassault Systèmes introduced DELMIA 3DLean in July which gives the **3D**EXPERIENCE platform a virtual white board for team collaboration. Eurostep's ShareAspace creates innovative and instantaneous collaboration spaces for complex supply chains. There are so many possibilities here that the cloud can enable that the only limit here will be our collective imagination.

Industrialization and Automation for Accelerating Deployments

Cloud vendors will continue to enhance their SaaS capabilities in order to address smaller companies and new, less PLM-experience markets. But for the larger companies with more than 200 users, Managed Services offerings will continue to be critical. PTC is planning to distribute Windchill via Kubernetes to allow for even easier deployment in cloud environments as well as enabling multi-tenant while still isolating code execution for each customer (or tenant). Aras Innovator is likely to introduce a SaaS model in the near term as well and enhance their cloud deployment capabilities accordingly. All the vendors acknowledge that one of the primary motivators of moving to cloud is reducing the deployment time and complexity. We will certainly see the solutions become even easier to deploy with less and less compromise necessary on adapting the solution to business needs in ways that require little or no programming which will accelerate deployment time and reduce both cost and risk.

---

[48] https://www.ptc.com/en/products/vuforia/vuforia-chalk
[49] https://www.slideshare.net/StephanClambaneva/if-only-da-vinci-had-an-augmented-reality-headset
[50] https://carbon3d.com

Self-Assessment Questions

Here are some of the questions that customers should ask themselves when considering cloud for PLM:

1. Is my vendor offering the identical or functionally equivalent portfolio on-premises as they are on the cloud or are there significant differences?
2. Are all upgrades handled transparently by the PLM vendor and do I have any control over when they are made?
3. How is my data secured from that of other customers hosted in the same PLM cloud?
4. How much flexibility does the PLM vendor offer me on the cloud in terms of adding my own attributes, implementing my own triggers and workflows, and modifying the user interface to be in ideal harmony with my existing tools?
5. Does the PLM vendor have a full set of integrations and web services so that my data can be moved seamlessly into and out of the system?
6. Can my existing PLM platform be easily migrated into the cloud or do I need to start from scratch?
7. If I am unhappy with my cloud journey and wish to move back on-premises, is this even possible with my cloud-based system, i.e., am I protected from vendor lock-in? And do I have plans to maintain hardware and skills in-house in case of a disruptive event that requires me to bring everything back on-premises?
8. Does the cloud PLM take into account the complexities of my supply chain and my need to exchange data with them and integrate them into my internal processes while safeguarding my IP?
9. Do I need to reduce my vision of implementation to fit the current cloud PLM's capabilities and do I trust the vendor to deliver on promises of future enhancements that will allow me to pursue my entire vision?
10. Will my users be ready to accept a new set of collaboration tools or will I face resistance to change that will need to be added as a risk factor in my implementation plans?

Conclusion, or PLM and Cloud post-COVID

As our world changes due to the COVID pandemic and we adjust to the new normal, using technology to facilitate social distancing while maintaining productivity, and promoting collaboration is an absolutely critical challenge. Cloud computing opens the door to efficient, secure remote working and collaboration and PLM allows the massive transformation of manual development processes into digital threads and digital twins. Currently, the market has a wide variety of offers which have been discussed in this white paper alongside discussions of cloud strengths and weaknesses.

The combination of the Cloud and PLM can be a tipping point for companies on their digital journey as they automate manual processes and accelerate their time to innovation and their time to market. However, as Shakespeare once wrote,

> "CALIBAN: The clouds methought would open and show riches
> Ready to drop upon me, that when I waked
> I cried to dream again."
>
> William Shakespeare <u>The Tempest</u>, Act 2, scene ii

Being open-eyed about the constraints and limitations of cloud will help to make the best decision for your business and avoid a reality that falls disappointingly short of your dreams.

I hope this book was helpful and got you to think a bit more deeply about Cloud and PLM.

Finocchiaro Consulting is here to help in case you need consulting or advice on moving forward.

About the Author

Michael Finocchiaro has been in PLM for the past 25+ years working for leaders such as IBM, HP, PTC and Dassault Systèmes. He is a respected leader in PLM Architectures as well as an expert on PLM and Cloud having been deeply involved in the launch of Dassault's **3D**EXPERIENCE platform on DS Public Cloud from 2014 to 2017. In 2017, he created Finocchiaro Consulting in order to help customers realize maximum benefit from their implementations of digital twins, and ensure the continuity of their digital threads. This white paper was realized in the context of an ongoing series of webcasts with his partner Haig&Co about the impacts of cloud computing on the Product Lifecycle Management market starting in Fall 2020. LinkedIn profile: https://www.linkedin.com/in/mfinocchiaro.

9 782955 983829